THE SECOND COMMAND

Building Midlife Wealth Command OS

Paolo Crisp

Copyright & Publication Notice

The Second Command:
Building Midlife Wealth Command Operating System (OS)

Author: Paolo Crisp
Copyright Holder: Paolo Crisp
Edition: First Edition
Publication Date: 2026

***

Copyright Notice

***

Disclaimer

Not Professional Advice: This book contains the author's personal perspectives and strategies for educational purposes only. It is not financial, legal, or tax advice. Consult qualified professionals in your jurisdiction before making financial decisions.

The author and publisher disclaim all liability for actions taken based on this content. Financial markets involve risk; past results don't guarantee future outcomes.

"THE SECOND COMMAND" and "WEALTH COMMAND OPERATING SYSTEM" are trademarks of Paolo Crisp.

***

Publishing Details

Published Globally Through: Amazon KDP, Barnes & Noble Press, Kobo Writing Life, Apple Books, and other international platforms.

Printing Locations: Various global facilities via print-on-demand services.

***

Contact

Rights & Permissions:
Email: squareholding1@gmail.com

Author Contact:
For media: squareholding1@gmail.com
Speaking inquiries: squareholding1@gmail.com

***

"Wealth is commanded, not created. Take command."

Paolo Crisp

Description

Your first command prepared you to follow orders. Your second command requires you to write them.

Alex Rivera had not penciled this into his five-year plan. Standing alone in the beige office at fifty-two, contemplating a severance agreement that read less like a document and more like a white flag.

Twenty-six years of service. Special Operations Command. Deployments across three continents. A chest of medals that now felt like borrowed artifacts; polished and impressive. They seemed entirely unrelated to the man holding them at this stage of life.

He had been trained to extract hostages, secure embassies, and plan missions where failure was not an option. He had not, however, been trained to extract himself from a corporate "soft landing." The phrase was delightful, like calling a parachute that never opens 'a gentle descent.' There was no landing. Only a slow, carpeted tumble, measured in quarterly reports and the gentle erosion of purpose.

The letter called it "strategic downsizing." His savings account murmured a more candid translation: Eighteen months until impact.

This was not the brochure. He had followed every instruction perfectly. Maxed the 401(k). Acquired the suburban fortress. Funded the higher education of his children. Listened intently to advisors who spoke of "diversification" and "horizons" as though wealth were a sunset to be admired, not a tool to be carried.

He traded camouflage for khaki, command for consensus, and mission-driven clarity for meetings, that could have been emails. His reward was a silent, paid-off home, a museum of milestones, where the only sound was the quiet hum of a refrigerator full of condiments for a life that was no longer happening.

He had followed the map. It led him to a very nice cul-de-sac at the edge of relevance.

Then, his phone lit up. A number from a buried past:
Heard you're at liberty? The Bunker. 1900. Bring your mind, not your resume – JD.

General James "JD" Donovan. Retired Joint Chief. The man who once told him, "We don't rise to the occasion. We default to our training." The man believed in systems over heroics.

What followed was not a new job. It was a new mission.

It was an answer to the question he hadn't dared ask out loud: what comes after the career is over, but the man is not?

It was about building a second life, not with more meetings, but with more meaning. Not with a bigger title, but with truer sovereignty. This was for the man whose wisdom exceeded his wealth, whose experience outpaced his time, and whose final ambition was to build something that would outlast him. Something no committee could ever vote to eliminate.

***

'The Second Command' is the story of that recalibration. It's the narrative journey of accomplished professionals discovering that everything they've been taught about money, retirement, and wealth is either incomplete, outdated, or deliberately misleading. Through Alex's eyes, and the unconventional mentorship of JD, the strategic genius of former intelligence analyst Maya Chen, and the disruptive energy of tech entrepreneur Sanjay Mehta; readers will discover that wealth creation after forty-five has less to do with financial products and everything to do with military-grade strategy.

This isn't a book about picking stocks or finding tax loopholes. It's about building what JD calls "The Wealth Command OS". An operating system that treats your financial life with the same strategic rigor as a military campaign. It's about understanding that diversification is what you do when you don't know where the enemy is. That risk management isn't about hiding from danger, but advancing through it, strategically. That your greatest asset isn't your investment portfolio, it's the experienced judgment you've earned through decades of leading, deciding, and surviving.

Part thriller, part masterclass, and entirely unconventional, 'The Second Command' takes readers from the boardrooms to the secure briefing rooms of Pentagon retirees, from failed ventures that felt like financial ambushes to strategic breakthroughs that built genuine sovereignty. It's for everyone who's finished their first career and realized the map they were given doesn't show the territory ahead. For leaders who understand that midlife isn't a decline; it's the high ground. And that the wealth worth building isn't measured in dollars, but in freedom, legacy, and command.

Your first command is over. Your second command begins here.

Dedication

This book is for the quiet professionals.

For the ones who spent decades following orders before realizing the most important orders would need to come from within. For the officers who traded uniforms for suits and discovered the corporate battlefield had different rules but the same stakes. For the entrepreneurs who built their first ventures like they were storming beaches, only to realize the real war was for sustainability, not just territory.

It's for my brothers and sisters in arms who came home and found that home had changed. Who discovered that transitioning from service doesn't mean abandoning mission, it means redefining it. Who looked at their medals and wondered, "What now?" and didn't find easy answers in the brochures from the Transition Assistance Office.

It's for the mid-career leaders who woke up at 3 AM with the unsettling realization that they're climbing someone else's ladder, toward someone else's definition of success. Who have the corner office, but not the corner on freedom. Who have the title but not the sovereignty.

For Maya, who taught me that intelligence isn't just about gathering information, but about discerning patterns in the noise. For Sanjay, who showed me that disruption isn't a buzzword, it's a survival tactic. For JD, who proved that retirement isn't an ending, but a redeployment.

For every reader who's accumulated experience like ammunition but hasn't been shown how to aim it. Who knows they have more to offer than their current mission requires. Who suspects there's a gap between what they've achieved and what they're capable of achieving, and that the bridge across that gap isn't made of motivation, but of systems.

This is for my family, who endured the absences of my first command and championed the emergence of my second. Who understood that sometimes coming home physically isn't the same as arriving home intentionally.

And for you, holding this book right now, wondering if it's too late or if you're too old, or if the systems are too stacked against you. It's not. You're not. They are, but that's why we need better systems.

This book is my after-action report. May it become your operations order.

Epigraph: The Doctrine of Sovereign Wealth

"Victorious warriors win first and then go to war, while defeated warriors go to war first and then seek to win."
— Sun Tzu, The Art of War

The wealthy build their fortune before they need it, constructing systems that generate sovereignty while others are still trading time for money. The financially defeated chase returns after losses, seek security after exposure, and build foundations during storms. True wealth is not won in the battle of markets; it is secured in the preparation between battles. Your financial victory was decided not by your last investment, but by the operating system you built years before the opportunity or crisis arrived.

***

"Risk comes from not knowing what you're doing."
— Warren Buffett

But danger comes from believing you know, when you don't. The financial industry sells certainty where none exists, products promising predictable returns in an inherently unpredictable world. Wealth creation at the sovereign level isn't about eliminating risk; it's about understanding it so completely that you can advance through volatility while others retreat. Your experience is your intelligence agency. Your judgment is your special operations team. Deploy them before you deploy your capital.

***

"The best investment you can make is in yourself."
— Charlie Munger

Yet most professionals invest in everything, but their own strategic education. They buy stocks instead of understanding markets. They purchase real estate without mastering leverage. They diversify across asset classes they cannot command. The most valuable territory in your wealth campaign is not in your portfolio; it's between your ears. Fortify your thinking before you fortify your balance sheet. Your mind is the command center from which all financial operations are launched.

***

"In the midst of chaos, there is also opportunity."
— Sun Tzu

Financial chaos is not an anomaly; it is the terrain. Market crashes, inflationary periods, geopolitical shifts, technological disruptions, these are not exceptions to be feared, but landscapes to be mapped and mastered. The greatest wealth transfers occur not during stability, but during volatility. While others see chaos, sovereign wealth builders see topography. While others seek shelter, strategists identify high ground. Your experience navigating complex systems is your topographic map through financial uncertainty.

***

"Amateurs talk tactics. Professionals talk logistics."
— Attributed to various military commanders

Financial amateurs debate stocks versus crypto, real estate versus bonds, active versus passive management. Wealth professionals design capital deployment systems, risk logistics frameworks, and resource supply chains. Your portfolio is not a collection of investments; it is a theater of operations. Each asset class is a different terrain requiring different logistics, different support lines, different extraction strategies. Master the movement of your resources, and the destination reveals itself.

***

"Do not put your trust in money but put your money in trust."
— Oliver Wendell Holmes, Sr.

Wealth is not the accumulation of currency; it is the construction of systems that generate sovereignty. Money in a bank account is potential energy. Money in a strategic operating system is kinetic power. The trust is not in the institution holding your assets, but in the intelligence governing their deployment. Build systems so robust that they generate freedom regardless of market conditions, so resilient that they withstand both predicted risks and Black Swan events, so adaptive that they evolve as you do.

***

"The supreme art of war is to subdue the enemy without fighting."
— Sun Tzu

The highest form of wealth creation renders competition irrelevant. Not by out-earning, but by out-thinking. Not by taking bigger risks, but by designing better systems. Sovereign wealth isn't built in the public markets where millions compete for fractional advantages; it's built in the private intersections of your unique experience, your proprietary networks, and your disciplined execution.

***

"It's not whether you're right or wrong that's important, but how much money you make when you're right and how much you don't lose when you're wrong."
— George Soros

Financial victory is not measured in being correct, but in being positioned. The market is not a test of intelligence; it is a theater of probabilities. Your strategy should not depend on perfect prediction, but on resilient positioning. Design systems that capture asymmetric upside while defining bounded downside. Build portfolios that profit from being right and survive being wrong. Wealth is not the reward for being correct; it is the outcome of superior positioning.

***

"Plans are worthless, but planning is everything."
— Dwight D. Eisenhower

Your financial plan will not survive by itself, it mat be far away from reality. Your children will choose unexpected paths. Your health will surprise you. Markets will defy predictions. Technologies will disrupt industries. The value of planning is not in the document produced, but in the strategic thinking developed, the scenarios considered, the flexibility designed into the system. The plan is not the destination; the planning is the navigation system that recalculates when the road disappears.

***

"Wealth consists not in having great possessions, but in having few wants."
— Epictetus

Yet sovereignty consists not in wanting less, but in commanding more; more freedom, more options, more impact, more legacy. The objective is not austerity, but autonomy. Not minimalism, but mastery. The wealth worth building, expands your command over your time, your choices, and your contribution. It is measured not in net worth statements, but in the quality of problems you get to solve and the scale of impact you get to create.

***

These principles are forming the doctrinal foundation of sovereign wealth creation. They represent not opposing philosophies, but complementary dimensions of the same strategic reality. Military precision provides the discipline.

Financial wisdom provides the opportunity. Personal sovereignty provides the purpose. Together, they form an operating system for building wealth that doesn't just accumulate, but commands.

Turn the page when you're ready, to stop collecting financial advice and start building wealth doctrine.

The Author

Paolo Crisp doesn't look like a revolutionary. At fifty-nine, with salt-and-pepper hair and the measured bearing of someone who's made decisions with consequences, he looks exactly like what he is: someone who's commanded in two worlds and discovered they're the same world, just wearing different uniforms.

His first command began not on a battlefield, but in the intricate, high-stakes world of the Navy. He wasn't just managing systems; he was architecting the nervous system of the world's fourth-largest maritime force. The budgets were measured in billions, the teams in hundreds, and the stakes in national security through strategic foresight. He learned that in military procurement, every decimal point has a consequence, every delay has a cost, and every system is only as strong as its weakest protocol.

Then came the pivot that nobody saw coming, least of all, him.

His second command played out not on warships, but in the volatile waters of North American businesses. From corporate enterprise roles to acquiring businesses and launching new startup ventures. He discovered that the corporate world had its own rules of engagement. He built channels, negotiated partnerships, and discovered that business, like warfare, is ultimately about understanding terrain and deploying resources with precision.

What emerged from these dual commands wasn't just a resume. It was a revelation: The same principles that secure nations can secure fortunes. The same discipline that manages billion-dollar defense budgets can optimize seven-figure business operations. The same strategic thinking that plans multi-year military infrastructure can build multi-generational wealth.

Today, Sid speaks to what he calls "the bilingual leaders", professionals who've succeeded in one domain but sense they're speaking only half the language of true sovereignty. He considers himself a systems architect. His mission isn't to inspire, but to equip. Not to motivate, but to systematize.

When he's not writing, speaking, or consulting, he's usually doing one of three things: hiking the trails of British Columbia (where he now lives), studying historical military campaigns for their strategic patterns, or having long dinners with his family where the conversation ranges from philosophy to finance to what makes a life worth commanding.

He wrote this book because he grew tired of seeing accomplished leaders with decades of experience following financial advice designed for beginners. Because he watched veterans transition from service to uncertainty when they should be transitioning from command to sovereignty. Because he believes your second act shouldn't be a decline from your first, it should be its strategic evolution.

This book is his field manual from the frontier between two worlds. Consider it your briefing for what comes next.

A Note on The Journey Ahead

This isn't a book you read. It's a book you deploy.

What you hold in your hands started as an after-action report, a collection of lessons learned across two careers, three countries, and what feels like a dozen lifetimes. It became something else: an operations order for the most important mission of your life.

But let's be clear about what you're getting into.

This isn't a traditional business book. You won't find ten easy steps to riches. You won't get motivational platitudes about thinking positively. You won't see a single pyramid scheme, get-rich-quick promise, or suggestion that wealth is about working harder than everyone else.

What you will find is a story. A narrative about people who look a lot like you, accomplished, experienced, capable, but sensing that something's missing from the financial map they've been given. You'll meet Alex Rivera, who's about to discover that everything he knows about planning is about to be tested. You'll encounter General JD Donovan, who understands that the best plans seem obvious once they've worked for you, but when you first hear them, they sound completely wrong. You'll learn from Maya Chen, who knows that intelligence isn't about having all the answers, but about asking better questions. And you'll witness Sanjay Mehta, who proves that sometimes the way forward isn't through the front door, but through the walls.

Through their journey, you'll be introduced to something called 'The Wealth Command OS', a systematic approach to wealth creation, that treats your financial life with the same strategic rigor as a military campaign. But here's the important part; the story culminates with an architecture of operating system for you, as we see it today. This is going to change eventually.

Let me explain.

This book contains the story, the philosophy, the strategic framework, the narrative proof of concept. The actual models, templates, calculators, briefing documents, and deployment tools, what we're calling 'The Digital Annex', which live at the end of this book. You will also have access to our evolving operating system as we move our miles in life through our website. This is every evolving and constantly maneuvering with the changing landscape of the terrain. That is because a static book can't contain a living operating system.

Think of it this way: This book is your officer training. The Digital Annex is your field kit. You need both, but they serve different purposes. Do you agree?

As you move through the chapters, you'll notice something unusual: There are no prescriptive "how-to" sections in the narrative. When Alex develops a capital deployment strategy, you won't get the spreadsheet. You'll get the thinking behind it. When Maya creates a risk assessment framework, you won't get the checklist. You'll get the philosophy that generated it.

This approach serves two purposes. First, it keeps the narrative flowing like the thriller it is, rather than the textbook it isn't. Second, and more importantly, it emphasizes that wealth creation at this level isn't about following someone else's recipe, it's about understanding the principles well enough to write your own.

Some chapters will feel like revelations. Some will feel like confrontations. All of them are designed to do one thing: Change how you think, about what's possible in the second half of your financial life.

A few guidelines as you begin:

1. Read in sequence. The Wealth Command OS builds module by module. Jumping ahead is like reading the extraction plan before understanding the insertion strategy.

2. Take notes in the margins, if you want. This is your briefing document. Interact with it. Challenge it. Make it yours.

3. When you reach end, go through the framework 'The Digital Annex' and pause. Explore the tools. Take what resonates. Ignore what doesn't. This system is modular by design.

4. Look for the patterns, not just the plot. The story carries the strategy. The characters demonstrate the principles. Your job isn't to memorize their decisions, but to understand their decision-making frameworks.

5. Prepare for cognitive discord. Some of this will contradict what you've been taught about money, retirement, and wealth. That's by design. Unlearning is the first phase of retraining.

This journey transformed everyone who lived it, in these pages. My hope is that it does the same for you. Not by giving you answers, but by upgrading the way you ask questions. Not by mapping your route, but by teaching you how to navigate.

Your first command taught you how to execute. Your second command begins with understanding what's worth executing.

Turn the page when you're ready to deploy.

***

Note: All character names, organizations, and specific events in this narrative have been fictionalized to protect operational security while preserving strategic truth. The systems, however, are real. And the invitation is genuine.

Table of Content

Prologue: The Extraction Protocol

Location: The Hindu Kush, Afghanistan | Altitude: 6,000 Feet | Time: 0230 Local

The night smelled of diesel, cordite, and the sharp, metallic flavour of fear.

Captain Alex Rivera lay flat on a ridge of rock and slate stone; his cheek pressed against the cold Picatinny rail of his sniper rifle. Below him, in a valley carved out of shadow and moonlight, sat the target: a compound that housed a regional warlord who had made the mistake of kidnapping three aid workers.

"Two minutes to extraction," the voice in his ear said. It was JD, General James Donovan, calm, detached, as if they were discussing a tee time rather than a life-or-death raid.

"Copy that," Alex whispered. "Package is secure. Team is mounted."

Alex scanned the sector. His mind wasn't just seeing the terrain; he was reading it. He saw the egress routes, the kill boxes, the lines of sight. He saw the logistics of violence. In twenty-six years of service, he had learned a fundamental truth of warfare: Amateurs talk strategy; professionals talk logistics. You could have the best tactics in the world, but if your fuel, your ammo, or your timing didn't align with the physics of the battlefield, you are dead.

"Captain, we have a heat signature moving up the southern draw," his spotter, Sergeant Miller, whispered. "Twelve contacts. Fast movers."

Alex adjusted his scope. The enemy was reacting. They were trying to cut off the extraction.

"Command," Alex said, his voice steady. "Requesting permission to divert. If we stay on the main road, the convoy is a sitting duck."

"Negative, Captain," JD replied instantly. "The heavy lift choppers are already inbound on that vector. You divert; you miss the ride."

"If we stay, we risk the package."

"Calculate the probability," JD said.

Alex didn't need a calculator. He had a supercomputer for a brain, hardwired by two decades of chaos management. Southern draw: high risk, high reward. Main road: moderate risk, dependence on air support.

Doctrine of Force Preservation: A commander must never risk his force unless the gain outweighs the cost. But here, the cost was innocent lives.

"Diverting," Alex said, disobeying the order. "We're taking the goat path. It's tight, but it offers natural cover."

Silence on the net for three seconds. Three seconds of judgment. Then, JD's voice returned, softer. "Understood. I'm redirecting the birds to the valley floor. You have a twelve-minute window to make the ridge line before they leave with or without you. Don't be late, Alex."

The next ten minutes were a blur of dust, roaring engines, and the sickening thud of rounds hitting the armored plating of their vehicle. Alex drove with the precision of a surgeon, threading the massive MRAP between boulders that scraped the paint off the doors. He wasn't driving; he was flowing. He was managing variables; speed, friction, gravity, like a conductor leading a symphony of violence.

They crested the ridge just as the Chinook helicopters flared into the wind, their rotors beating the air into submission. Alex drove the vehicle straight into the open bay ramp, the tires squealing on the metal mesh. The ramp closed, sealing out the war.

As the helicopter lifted, banking away from the tracer fire, rising from the valley like angry fireflies, Alex slumped back in his seat. His heart rate was 110. Not bad. He checked his team. Everyone was breathing. The package was safe.

He exhaled. It was a perfect extraction. Flawless logistics. Superior intelligence.

He didn't know it then, but it was the last time he would ever feel that competent.

***

Location: The Pentagon | Arlington, Virginia | Three Months Later

The transition from a dusty ridge in Afghanistan to the polished, climate-controlled sterility of the Pentagon, wasn't just a change of geography; it was a dimensional shift.

Alex stood in a secure briefing room on the E-Ring. It smelled of stale coffee and floor wax. He wore his Class A uniform, the medals on his chest heavy with history.

The screen at the front of the room didn't show topographical maps or enemy dispositions. It showed a spreadsheet. A red line sloping downward.

"Captain Rivera," said the man in the suit. His name was Mr. Henderson from the Office of Personnel Management. He looked like a human resources manager for a funeral home. "We're here to discuss your transition strategy."

"My transition strategy," Alex repeated. "Sir, with all due respect, I'm overseeing a logistics realignment for the Indo-Pacific theater."

"Not anymore," Henderson said, sliding a folder across the mahogany table. "Effective in ninety days, you are being retired. Or, as we like to say, extruded from the force structure."

Alex stared at the folder. Extruded. Like toothpaste from a tube.

“I have two years left on my contract,” Alex said, his voice dropping an octave. The “Command Voice” was automatic.

Henderson didn’t flinch. He tapped the screen. “Budget cuts, Captain. We’re optimizing the force mix. We’re moving resources from personnel legacy systems to autonomous platforms. You...” He hesitated, searching for a euphemism. “You are a legacy system.”

The words hit Alex harder than a roadside bomb. Legacy system. Obsolete. Rusty.

“What about my mission?” Alex asked. “The Indo-Pacific supply chain security?”

“Will be handled by algorithms and drones,” Henderson said cheerfully. “It’s more efficient. You understand efficiency. You’re a logistics man.”

The meeting dragged on. Henderson talked about pension vesting schedules, healthcare conversions, and the Thrift Savings Plan rollover process. He used words like "downsizing" and "rightsizing" as if he were talking about clothing, not men who had bled for their country.

But Alex wasn’t listening. He was experiencing a System Failure.

In the military, when a system fails, you initiate a Contingency Operation. You switch to backup power. You reroute through alternate nodes. You fight your way out.

But here? In this fluorescent-lit box? There was no fight. There was only paperwork.

When the meeting finally ended, Henderson shook his hand with a grip like a dead fish. "Good luck, Captain; and remember, you've earned your rest."

Alex walked out of the Pentagon and into the humid Virginia afternoon. He sat on a bench overlooking the Potomac River. He watched the boats moving on the water, tugs, barges, sailboats. They all had a destination. They all had a purpose.

He took off his hat and ran a hand through his hair. He looked at his reflection in the dark glass of the building.

For twenty-six years, he had been an Operator. A man who made things happen in the dark, so others could live in the light. He had managed billions of dollars of equipment, commanded thousands of lives, and made decisions that shifted the geopolitical tectonic plates.

Now, he is forced to be a "civilian."

He stood up. He looked at the Pentagon, the massive fortress of stone and concrete. It had been his first command. His first life.

He reached into his pocket and found a marker. On the back of the financial brochure, he wrote a single word in thick, black letters:

SOVEREIGNTY

Then he circled it twice.

He didn't know how yet. He didn't know where the resources would come from or who the allies were. But he knew one thing: The war wasn't over. He had just been reassigned to a new theater of operations.

And this time, the objective was personal.

Part I: The Awakening

(The Trap Is Sprung)

Chapter 1: The Peace Dividend Illusion

The next early morning at his home.

He pulled a folded piece of paper from his pocket. It was a brochure from a financial advisor named Martin. Elena, his wife, had made the appointment. "He comes highly recommended," she had said. "He specializes in military transitions."

Alex opened the brochure. On the cover, a silver-haired couple sat on a beach, holding hands. The caption read: The Glide Path to Serenity.

He looked at the couple's peaceful faces. They looked bored. They looked... dead inside.

Alex realized with a cold, creeping dread that the military wasn't the only organization that practiced "extraction."

The financial world wanted to extract him, too. They wanted to take his accumulated capital, his pension, his experience, and grind it down into manageable, predictable fees, for them. They wanted to put him on a glide path.

But Alex Rivera didn't glide. He didn't descend. He ascended. He assaulted objectives.

***

Location: McLean, Virginia | 10:00 AM

The office of Martin Sterling, Certified Financial Planner, smelled of vanilla potpourri and expensive calmness. It was the kind of silence that cost $300 an hour to maintain.

Alex sat in a chair that was designed to swallow him whole, soft leather, deep cushioning, angled to induce a state of relaxed helplessness. He wore a civilian suit, navy blue, off the rack. It felt like a costume. He missed the weight of the body armor. At least armor protected you; this suit just made you look like you were trying too hard.

Martin sat behind a desk the size of an aircraft carrier. He was a man of sixty, with a tan that suggested regular visits to places where taxes were low, and drinks were served in coconuts. He smiled the kind of smile that had been practiced in a mirror.

"Alex," Martin said, spreading his hands. "Welcome to the next chapter. Your honorable discharge was the start of something wonderful. The Peace Dividend."

Alex looked at the screen on the wall. It displayed a line graph. A green line went up, then flattened out, then gently sloped downward like a skier coming down a bunny hill.

"The Glide Path," Martin said, tapping the screen with a laser pointer. "This is the industry gold standard for someone with your risk profile."

"And what is my risk profile?" Alex asked. His voice was flat. He was using his Interrogation Voice.

Martin chuckled. "Conservative. Prudent. You're entering the preservation phase, Alex. You've spent thirty years accumulating capital. Now, you need to switch from Offense to Defense. From Asset Accumulation to De-accumulation."

De-accumulation. The word sounded like a medical condition.

"Explain the math," Alex said.

Martin brightened. He loved the math. It was his shield. "We take your pension, your severance, your TSP, and your 401(k). We roll them into a managed portfolio. Based on the Four Percent Rule, the Trinity Study, 1998, we calculate that you can withdraw 4% of your principal annually, adjusted for inflation, with a 95% probability of the money lasting thirty years."

Alex did the mental arithmetic. It wasn't hard. He had calculated artillery trajectories in his head while under fire.

"So," Alex said, "I get to live on the equivalent of a Lieutenant Colonel's salary until I die. And if I die early, the unspent money goes to... who?"

Martin hesitated. "Well, to your heirs. Or to charity. Or back to the state in estate taxes."

"Or" Alex said, leaning forward, the leather chair creaking, "I could die early, and the financial industry keeps the management fees on the principal I never spent."

Martin's smile tightened. "That's a rather cynical way to look at it."

"I'm not cynical. I'm a logistics officer," Alex said. "I look at flow. You're telling me that for the next thirty years, I should restrict my operational capacity to a fixed ration. That I should accept a declining influence. That I should... what? Garden?"

Martin laughed, a short, barking sound. "Alex, you've earned the right to garden. You've been shot at. You've managed wars. Don't you want to rest? The 'Peace Dividend' is the reward for service."

Alex looked at the green line. The Glide Path.

He saw a different picture. He didn't see a path to serenity. He saw a Kill Box.

Doctrine: Defilade. Military units use defilade, using the terrain to protect themselves from enemy observation and fire.

Martin was offering Alex financial defilade. He was telling him to hide in a hole, keep his head down, and hope the artillery of inflation, market crashes, and healthcare costs didn't land on him.

But there was a fundamental flaw in the doctrine.

"Major General Donovan used to say something," Alex said softly. "He said, 'If you're on the defensive, you're already losing. The only way to win is to dictate the terms of the engagement.'"

Martin looked confused. "Is that from Sun Tzu, The Art of War?"

"It's from the school of hard knocks," Alex said. "Martin, this chart... this assumes my income stops. It assumes my value to the market drops to zero the day I take off the uniform."

Martin checked his watch. He was a busy man. He had other fish to gently fry. "Alex, the market doesn't care about your feelings. It cares about statistics. And statistically, older people are less productive, more expensive to insure, and less adaptable. The Glide Path manages that reality."

Less adaptable.

Alex felt a familiar heat in his chest. It was the same heat he felt when a junior officer suggested a route through a valley that hadn't been explored. It was the heat of Contradiction.

He stood up. The movement was sudden, violent in its stillness. Martin flinched.

"I'm not going to garden, Martin," Alex said. "And I'm not going to glide."

"Alex, the window for the penalty-free rollover closes in—"

"I know the window," Alex snapped. "I know the Rules of Engagement." He turned and walked to the door. He stopped with his hand on the knob. "Do you know what happens to an army that stops advancing, Martin?"

Martin blinked. "No."

"They get surrounded. And then they get slaughtered."

Alex walked out.

***

Location: The Bunker | Arlington, Virginia | 2:00 PM

The Bunker was not on any map. It occupied the third floor of a converted textile warehouse in a part of Arlington where the restoration had stopped abruptly, leaving a frontier of auto-body shops and taquerias.

Alex punched the code into the keypad; 2-6-1-7, the date of the Battle of Trenton, Washington's crossing. The heavy steel door clicked and swung open.

The air inside was different. It smelled of ozone, solder, and dark roast coffee. It didn't smell like a business. It smelled like a Command Center.

"Status," Alex said, walking into the room.

“Market is down 120 points on geopolitical jitters,” a voice said from behind a wall of six monitors. “Crypto is up. Gold is flat. And you look like you want to punch someone.”

It was Maya Chen. She was twenty-eight, wore a hoodie that said CTRL+ALT+DEL, and had eyes that scanned data streams the way Alex used to scan for IEDs.

“Martin offered me a glide path,” Alex said, tossing his jacket onto a crate of server equipment.

“And you didn’t take it?” Another voice. Sanjay Mehta rolled out from under a desk on a mechanic’s-creeper. He was holding a soldering iron like a weapon. He was thirty, wore sneakers, with open laces, and had founded three tech companies. Eventually, he had sold these companies for numbers that made Alex’s head spin.

“I told him to shove his Peace Dividend,” Alex said.

“Excellent,” Sanjay said, sitting up and wiping grease on his jeans. “Peace is bad for business. Chaos is a ladder.”

Alex walked to the center of the room. The main screen, a massive eighty-inch display, was dark. “Where is JD?”

“He’s watching the Fed testimony,” Maya said, typing furiously. “He’ll be here in five minutes. But in the meantime,...” She pressed a key, and the main screen lit up.

It wasn’t a stock chart. It was a map.

It showed the United States, but instead of states, it was divided into color-coded zones. Red zones. Blue zones. Green zones.

"What is this?" Alex asked.

"Terrain analysis," Maya said. "JD told us to prepare for your arrival."

She pointed to a red zone covering the Midwest. "This is the Rust Belt. Demographic decline. Outbound migration. Financial death spiral."

She pointed to a blue zone in the Pacific Northwest. "Tech corridor. High growth, high velocity. But regulatory friction."

Then she pointed to a pulsing green zone right over their heads. "Northern Virginia. The Defense Industrial Complex surrounding Techno Intelligence Complex. This is the richest soil in the country, Alex. And you're standing right in."

Alex looked at the map. He understood terrain. He understands that you didn't fight the terrain; you use it.

"Martin told me, I'm a legacy system," Alex said, staring at the green zone. "That I'm obsolete."

"Martin sells umbrellas," Sanjay said, standing up and walking over to the whiteboard. He picked up a marker. "He assumes it's always going to rain. So, he tells you to sit inside and wait for the sun. We develop seeds. We tell you to plant crops in the storm."

Sanjay drew a circle on the board. Inside, he wrote: CAPITAL.

"Money is ammunition," Sanjay said. "Martin thinks your ammunition is a limited resource that needs to be hoarded. We think ammunition is a resource that needs to be expended to gain territory."

"Fire and Maneuver," Alex murmured. The military doctrine of suppressing the enemy with fire (firepower) while moving troops (maneuver) to a better position.

"Exactly," Sanjay said. "Martin wants you to sit in the foxhole (the Glide Path) and hope the enemy runs out of bullets. We want you to use your capital to flank the market. To seize the high ground."

"Where is the high ground?" Alex asked.

"Real assets," Sanjay said. "Things that can't be printed. Businesses. Systems. Real estate. Intellectual Property. But most importantly..." He tapped Alex's chest. "Your experience."

The door at the back of the room opened. General JD Donovan walked in. He didn't wear a uniform anymore. He wore jeans and a denim shirt. But he still moved with the weight of a mountain.

"He tried to sell you the illusion," JD said by way of greeting. He walked to the coffee pot and poured a cup. Black. "The Peace Dividend."

"Yes, sir."

"The Peace Dividend is a lie, Alex," JD said, turning to face them. "It's a fairy tale they tell to keep the herd calm. They tell you that if you work hard for forty years, you get to stop. That the world will leave you alone."

JD walked to the screen. He looked at the map of the United States.

"But the world doesn't stop," JD continued. "Inflation is a tax. Market crashes are redistribution events. Currency devaluation is a confiscation of wealth. If you 'glide,' you're just drifting in a current that's pulling you over the waterfall."

"So, what's the alternative?" Alex asked. "I'm not a twenty-year-old coder. I can't build an app in my garage."

"Bingo," Maya said. "But you know how to command."

She pulled up a new file on the screen. It was a flowchart. It was incredibly complex. Inputs, outputs, feedback loops, gatekeepers.

"What is this?" Alex asked.

"This is the Wealth Command OS," Maya said. "The Operating System we're building for you. Not a financial plan. A command structure."

She pointed to the top box. COMMAND.

"Most civilians operate on a Democracy OS," she explained. "They argue with themselves. They want the Porsche, but they also want the retirement fund. They want safety, but they also want excitement. Their internal government is gridlocked."

Alex nodded. He knew soldiers like that. Indecisive. Dangerous.

"You need a Dictatorship OS," Maya said. "A benevolent dictator. Your brain. The OS separates your Strategic Mind from your Tactical Fear."

JD stepped closer to Alex. "Alex, do you remember the doctrine of Force Multiplier?"

"Yes, sir," Alex said. "A factor that dramatically increases the combat effectiveness of a unit. Like night vision, or air superiority."

"Your experience is your force multiplier," JD said. "Your network is your force multiplier. Your discipline is your force multiplier. You're trying to fight a financial war with just your capital (the ammo). But you have these massive force multipliers you aren't using."

He gestured to the room. "This team, Sanjay, Maya, me, we are your joint chiefs. We are your intelligence apparatus. We are the logistics corps."

"But what's the mission?" Alex asked. He needed a mission. Without a mission, he was just a man with a gun and no target.

JD put his coffee cup down. He looked Alex in the eye. The look was sharp, terrifying, and exhilarating.

"The mission, Alex, is Sovereignty. Total, absolute, financial sovereignty. The ability to say 'no' to anyone, anytime, for any reason. The ability to protect your family not from a physical threat, but from a systemic one."

JD walked to the whiteboard and wrote a date.

"Three months," JD said. "In three months, the market is going to correct. We see the signs. Liquidity is drying up. The algorithms are twitching. We are going into a recession."

Alex felt the hairs on his arms stand up. This wasn't theory. This was actionable intelligence.

"Martin will tell you to hunker down," JD said. "He will tell you to ride it out. That is the Peace Dividend Illusion."

JD drew an upward arrow on the board, defying the downward slope of the recession.

"We," JD said, "are going to attack."

"Attack?" Alex asked. "With what?"

"With your severance," JD said. "With your pension. With your home equity. We are going to consolidate your scattered assets into a strike force. And when the market bleeds, we are going to buy."

Alex looked at the map. He looked at the complex flowchart of the OS. He looked at the team of misfits and geniuses.

For the first time in three months, the static in his head cleared. The low-level hum of anxiety vanished, replaced by the sharp, clean frequency of focus.

This was a briefing.

He was the Commander.

And the war was just beginning.

"Tell me about the OS," Alex said, pulling a chair up to the war table. "I want to know the Kernel."

Maya smiled. It was a shark's smile. "Welcome to 'The Second Command', Alex. Boot up sequence starts now."

***

Lesson Learnt:

- Military Doctrine: Force Multiplication. A force multiplier is anything that increases the effectiveness of a weapon system or a unit. In finance, capital is the weapon, but strategy, experience, and networks are the multipliers. Using only money is like shooting blindly; using money plus strategy is a laser-guided missile.

- Financial Doctrine: Sovereignty vs. The Peace Dividend. The "Peace Dividend" implies that after work, you deserve rest. But financial entropy never sleeps. Sovereignty is the state of having supreme authority over your own economic fate, independent of external systems (like a pension or an employer). It requires constant vigilance and active command, not passive gliding.

Chapter 2: Sun Tzu In a Suit

Location: The Bunker | Arlington, Virginia | 09:00 Hours

The air in The Bunker was cold enough to preserve meat. Maya liked it that way; she claimed it kept the servers from overheating and kept her thinking sharp. Alex, still acclimating to civilian life, wore a fleece over his button-down, nursing a coffee that had gone lukewarm an hour ago.

On the main screen, a map of the world was spinning, but it didn't show borders. It showed fiber-optic cables, shipping lanes, and dark pool liquidity zones. It looked like a circulatory system for a giant, sleeping beast.

"Stop looking at the countries," Maya said without turning around. She was typing on a keyboard that clicked like a field of crickets. "Nations are obsolete. They are just administrative overlays on the real empire."

"And what is the real empire?" Alex asked, walking up to the screen.

"Flow," she said. "The movement of value."

Sanjay rolled his chair over, a bag of dried mangoes in one hand. "She's doing her Matrix impression again. What she means is, Alex, you're still thinking like a patriot. You think the U.S. economy is a team. It's not. It's an ecosystem. And in an ecosystem, the lion doesn't care if the gazelle is American or Canadian. The lion just eats."

JD walked in, carrying a battered hardcover book. He wore a blazer that had seen better decades, the leather elbows worn smooth. He placed the book on the central table with a heavy thud.

The Art of War. The ancient edition, the characters vertical and sharp.

"Yesterday, we talked about the mission," JD said, sitting down. "Sovereignty. But you cannot achieve sovereignty if you do not understand the battlefield. And you, Captain, are currently fighting on the wrong terrain."

Alex looked at the book. He had read it three times. It was standard reading for field grade officers. "Sun Tzu. Terrain. Weather. Moral law. I know the doctrine, General."

"Do you?" JD opened the book, the spine cracking with age. "Because the last time you looked at your 401(k), you didn't see terrain. You saw a casino. You saw a slot machine."

"That's what it is," Alex argued. "A gamble. You put money in, you hope it goes up."

Sanjay laughed, spraying crumbs of dried mango onto the floor. "That's what the house wants you to think. If you think it's a gamble, you focus on luck. You focus on the dice. You pray. But the house? The house isn't gambling. The house is running a logistics operation. They know the exact mathematical percentage they will win over time. They aren't playing. They're processing."

JD pointed to the screen. "Sun Tzu wrote, 'Know the enemy and know yourself; in a hundred battles, you will never be in peril.' The financial industry has inverted this. They tell you to know neither."

He stood up and walked to the whiteboard. He picked up a marker and drew a square. Inside the square, he drew a stick figure.

"Here is you," JD said. "Here is the retail investor. The civilian. You are standing in an open field."

Next to the stick figure, he drew a massive, fortress-like structure with turrets and high walls.

"Here is the institution. The hedge fund. The bank. They are behind the Maginot Line. They have armor. They have speed. They have information you don't have. They see the order flow a millisecond before you do."

Alex nodded. "So, I'm outgunned. That's why Martin told me to hide. To buy bonds and sit in the trench."

"The French built the Maginot Line after World War I," JD said, his voice dropping into a lecture cadence. "It was the ultimate defensive fortification. Impenetrable. Safe. The Germans didn't bother attacking it. They just flew over it. They went around it."

He drew a dotted line bypassing the fortress and striking deep into the unprotected rear.

"Martin is trying to sell you a spot inside the Maginot Line," JD continued. "He thinks safety is walls. He thinks safety is static defense. But the enemy, Inflation, Market Volatility, Technological Disruption, they aren't infantry. They are the Luftwaffe. They fly over walls."

Maya spun her chair around. "Alex, do you know what 'Alpha' is? In finance?"

"Excess return," Alex recited. "Beating the market."

"Wrong," Maya said sharply. "That's what they tell you. Alpha is actually Information. Asymmetry. It's knowing something the market hasn't priced in yet. The institutions have algorithms scraping Twitter, satellite imagery of parking lots, credit card transaction data. They have the intelligence advantage."

She tapped her screen. A complex web of red and blue lines appeared. It looked like a neural network.

"We are building an Intelligence Apparatus for you," Maya said. "We are going to find the terrain where the institutions cannot go. Where their size is a disadvantage, not an advantage."

"Where is that?" Alex asked.

"Small cap," Sanjay said. "Private equity. Distressed assets. Places where you can't deploy a billion dollars without moving the price. You can move five million dollars like a sniper. They have to move five billion like a tank. We're going to make you the sniper."

JD turned to a specific page in The Art of War. He read aloud. "'All warfare is based on deception.'"

"The financial industry loves that verse," Alex said. "Pump and dump schemes. Fraud."

"No," JD corrected. "That's criminal deception. Sun Tzu meant structural deception. 'Appear weak when you are strong. Appear strong when you are weak.' The market appears chaotic, random. It appears efficient. It is not."

He drew a bell curve on the board.

"This is the Normal Distribution," JD said. "The famous Bell Curve. It assumes market returns are random and predictable. It is the foundation of Modern Portfolio Theory. It is also the biggest lie ever told."

He took the eraser and wiped out the tails of the bell curve.

"Real life doesn't live in the middle," JD said. "Real life lives in the tails. The Black Swans. The crashes. The manias. The market spends 90% of its time boring you to death, and 10% of the time scaring you to death. The deception is that the 90% is the reality. It's not. The 10% is the reality."

Alex looked at the graph. He thought about his time in Afghanistan. 99% of the time was boredom, patrols, maintenance, waiting. 1% was pure terror. That 1% defined the war.

"So, you're saying," Alex said slowly, "that the 'Safe' portfolio is ignoring the 10%."

"It's assuming the 10% won't happen," Sanjay said. "It's assuming the hurricane won't hit because the weather has been nice for ten years. That's not strategy. That's wishful thinking."

JD closed the book. "We are not playing the probability game, Alex. We are playing the possibility game. We don't care what is likely to happen. We care about what happens if we are wrong."

Alex felt a shift in the room. The air seemed to thicken. This was the language he spoke. In the military, you didn't plan for the enemy to act logically. You planned for them to do the one thing you hoped they wouldn't do. You planned for the worst-case scenario because in war, the worst-case usually had a way of showing up.

"Show me the terrain," Alex said.

***

Location: Tyson's Corner, Virginia | 11:30 Hours

JD had sent Alex on a solo mission. A field exercise.

"Go look," he had said. "Don't buy. Don't sell. Just look."

Alex stood in the middle of the food court at Tyson's Corner Galleria. It was a cathedral of commerce. Three stories of glass and chrome. Teenagers swarmed the Apple Store; parents pushed strollers through the halls; businesspeople in suits tapped on phones.

To Alex, it didn't look like a mall. It looked like a supply depot.

He bought a pretzel and found a spot on the second-floor balcony overlooking the main atrium. He watched the flow of people. He tried to apply JD's lesson: Terrain and Flow.

He saw a kiosk selling phone cases. The vendor was shouting, waving a charger. High energy, low margins. That was Guerrilla Warfare.

He saw the Apple Store. Silent. People waiting in line to give money away. The products didn't need a sales pitch; the brand was the fortress. That was Air Superiority.

Then he saw a sign in the window of a high-end watch store. "50% Off Liquidation Sale."

Alex's military instincts tingled. Liquidation. Forced liquidation was a tactical failure. It meant you were out of ammo, out of time, and willing to take a loss just to survive the night. But for a buyer, a liquidation sale was an exploited weakness. It was a breach in the line.

He pulled out his phone and opened the stock trading app he had downloaded. He typed in the ticker symbol of the watch company.

The stock was down 40% for the year. News headlines scrolled across the screen: "Luxury Retail Struggles as Inflation Bites."

The herd was running. Fear.

Martin would have told him to stay away. "Why catch a falling knife?"

But Alex remembered the terrain. The store was in a prime location. The brand was heritage. The inventory was physical. The problem wasn't the product; the problem was the capital structure. They had too much debt.

If you bought the debt, you owned the company. If you owned the company, you owned the real estate. You controlled the terrain.

Alex didn't buy. He wasn't ready. But he watched.

He watched a young couple walk into the store. The boyfriend looked terrified; the girlfriend looked determined. They were buying a watch they couldn't afford, using a credit card with 24% interest.

Alex realized he wasn't just watching a transaction. He was watching a transfer of sovereignty. The couple was transferring their future freedom (labor) to the bank (capital) in exchange for a shiny object (status).

They were becoming employees of the bank.

And that's when he saw the enemy.

It wasn't a person. It wasn't a bank. It was the Design.

The mall was designed to make you walk past the pretzel shop, so you'd get hungry. It was designed to make the Apple Store look like a temple. It was designed to make the credit card feel like free money.

The enemy was the environment itself.

His phone buzzed. A text from Maya. Target identified?

Alex typed back: Visual confirmed. The civilians are walking into a kill box, and they don't even know there's a war on.

He watched the couple leave the store, the watch box clutched tightly. They were smiling. They thought they had won. They had the trophy.

Alex took a bite of his cold pretzel. It tasted like stale bread and enlightenment.

He remembered JD's voice: "To win without fighting is best."

The couple had fought. They had fought the urge to save. They had fought the math. They had spent hours agonizing over the decision. And they had lost. They had transferred their wealth to the system.

The strategic player, the one who owned the debt, or the mall landlord, or the credit card company, they hadn't fought. They had just set the terrain. They had built the trap.

And they had won before the couple even walked in the door.

***

Location: The Bunker | 02:00 PM

Alex returned to The Bunker to find the mood dark. The screens were flashing red. Sanjay was pacing, talking rapidly on the phone in a language Alex didn't recognize, Hindi? Farsi?

JD was staring at a single monitor, his face unreadable.

"What happened?" Alex asked, dropping his keys on the table.

"Intel update," Maya said quietly. "The market is twitching. A major hedge fund just blew up. Archegos Capital."

Alex looked at the screen. It showed a graph plummeting to zero. "They used leverage?" "Massive leverage," JD said. "They borrowed billions to bet on tech stocks. The banks pulled the rug. They're wiping out."

Billions of dollars. Gone in hours. Generations of wealth evaporated.

"This is what I was talking about," Alex said, pointing at the screen. "The 10%. The tail risk."

"Exactly," JD said. He looked at Alex. "Do you know who made money today?"

"The shorts?"

"The prime brokers," JD corrected. "The clearinghouses. The people who insured the terrain. The people who sold the shovels."

JD walked to the whiteboard. He wiped it clean and wrote two words:

FORCE PRESERVATION

"In the military, you never commit your reserves unless you are certain of victory," JD said. "Archegos committed everything. They bet the farm. They lost."

He pointed at Alex. "You, Alex, are the Reserve Force. You are not the front-line infantry getting chewed up in the daily machine gun fire of the market. You are the Special Ops team. You wait. You watch. You train."

"Until when?"

"Until the terrain favors the weapon," Sanjay said, hanging up his phone. He looked flushed. "The fund that collapsed? They were forced to sell their good assets to cover their bad debts. They are dumping blue-chip stocks at bargain prices just to raise cash."

"Fire sale," Alex said. "Just like the watch store."

"Yes," Sanjay said. "But on a global scale. This is the Deception, Alex. The news says, 'Market Panic.' The narrative is 'Danger.' The reality is... Opportunity."

JD nodded. "Sun Tzu said, 'Appear weak when you are strong.' The market appears weak today. The hedge fund is dead. The banks are scared. But the underlying value of the companies being sold hasn't changed. The terrain hasn't changed. Only the perception has."

He looked Alex in the eye. "This is the difference between a gambler and a commander. The gambler sees the red numbers and feels fear. The commander sees the red numbers and sees a breached wall."

Alex looked at the red charts. For the first time in his life, he didn't feel a pit in his stomach when he saw the arrows pointing down. He didn't feel the anxiety of the 401(k) dropping.

He felt... anticipation.

It was the feeling he used to get in the briefing room, looking at a satellite photo of a target compound. The feeling that comes right before the op goes down. The feeling of knowing that while everyone else was confused, you had the plan.

"So," Alex said, rolling up his sleeves. "How do we exploit the breach?"

JD smiled. It was a cold, calculated smile. A predator's smile. "We don't buy yet. We let them bleed a little more. We let them panic. We let the deception become complete."

He tapped the book. "'Let your plans be dark and impenetrable as night, and when you move, fall like a thunderbolt.'"

Alex looked at the screen. The red numbers were still falling. The panic was spreading. Somewhere, thousands of Martins were telling thousands of Alexes to stay the course, to ride it out, to think long term.

But here, in The Bunker, they weren't thinking about the long term. They were thinking about the kill.

And for the first time, Alex didn't feel like a retired soldier watching from the sidelines.

He felt like a sniper adjusting his scope.

The crosshairs were on the battlefield. He just had to wait for the wind to die down.

***

Lesson Learnt:

- Military Doctrine: Maginot Line Mentality. Static defense fails against dynamic threats. Building a "safe" wall (bonds/conservative funds) ignores the fact that the enemy (inflation/systemic risk) can simply fly over it. True defense requires mobility and the ability to counter-attack.

- Financial Doctrine: Information Asymmetry & Structural Deception. The market is not a casino; it is a battlefield of unequal information. The "House" (institutions) wins through structural advantages (speed, data, scale). The individual cannot beat them at their game (High Frequency Trading). The individual must win on terrain where the giant cannot tread, small, illiquid, or distressed opportunities, where judgment and experience outweigh algorithmic speed. Deception lies in the difference between price (the noise) and value (the terrain).

Chapter 3: Your First Command: A Debrief

Location: The Rivera Residence | Suburban Virginia | 06:00 Hours

The house was quiet. The kind of quiet that only exists in the moments before the world wakes up, a fragile ceasefire between sleep and chaos.

Alex sat at the kitchen island, the granite cold under his forearms. A pot of coffee brewed in the corner, ticking like a metronome. In front of him lay the "Terrain Assessment" document Maya had sent him. It was open on a tablet, the cursor blinking at the end of the first question.

“List the five most significant failures of your career. Not the outcomes. The decisions.”

Alex stared at the question. He rubbed his temples.

In the military, you did not dwell on failure. You did an After-Action Review (AAR), you wrote up the lessons learned in the official report, and then you archived it. You moved on to the next mission. To linger on a mistake was to invite doubt. Doubt got people killed.

But this document wasn't asking for a formal report. It was asking for a confession.

He took a sip of coffee. Black. Bitter.

Upstairs, the floorboards creaked. Elena was awake.

Alex minimized the document, instinctively hiding his screen. He felt ridiculous. He was a fifty-one-year-old man, hiding his homework from his wife like a teenager skipping calculus.

Elena came down the stairs a few minutes later, wearing her robe, her hair pulled back in a ponytail. She looked tired. She looked beautiful. She looked like the only reality that mattered.

"You're up early," she said, heading straight for the coffee maker.

"Couldn't sleep," Alex said.

"Thinking about the presentation?" she asked, pouring a cup.

"Yeah. The transition." It wasn't a lie. It just wasn't the whole truth.

Elena leaned against the counter, blowing on her mug. "Martin emailed me. He said you two had a... spirited discussion."

Alex frowned. "He called it spirited. I called it attempted murder."

"He says we're on a timeline, Alex. Something about rollovers and tax windows."

"We have time," Alex said, trying to keep his voice level. "Don't let him pressure you. That's how they sell annuities. Urgency."

Elena looked at him over the rim of her cup. Her eyes were sharp. She was a corporate lawyer; she knew when a witness was hedging.

"You've been weird lately," she said. "You're gone all day. You come back with whiteboard marker on your hands. You smell like solder and old coffee." She paused. "Are you having an affair?"

The question hit Alex like a flashbang. It was so absurd he almost laughed, but the look on her face stopped him. She wasn't joking. She was assessing a threat to the Home Front.

"No," he said quickly. "God, no. Elena, I promise you. There is no one else."

"Then what is it?" She walked over to the island. "Because you're not looking for a job. I've checked your LinkedIn. You haven't updated your profile. You're not networking. You're just... disappearing."

Alex looked at his wife. He wanted to tell her. He wanted to tell her about The Bunker, about JD, about the map of the world made of fiber-optic cables. He wanted to tell her about the war.

But he couldn't. The mission was compartmentalized. Until he had a plan, until he had a weapon, worry was just noise.

"I'm working on a project," he said finally. "A consulting gig. Pro bono, mostly. For an old mentor."

"Doing what?"

"Logistics," Alex said. "Systems analysis."

Elena sighed. She put a hand on his shoulder. "Alex, I love you. But you're retired. You don't have to save the world anymore. You just have to help me get the kids to soccer practice and figure out how we're going to pay for college in six years."

She walked out of the kitchen, leaving her coffee on the counter.

Alex sat alone again. The silence had changed. It wasn't peaceful anymore. It was heavy.

He opened the tablet again.

"List the five most significant failures."

He typed: 2014. Kandahar. The Supply Convoy.

He remembered it vividly. He was a Major then. He had authorized a convoy to move fuel through a valley that intel said was clear. It wasn't. An IED took out the lead truck. Two soldiers injured. No one died, thank God, but the mission was scrubbed. The fuel never made it to the Forward Operating Base.

The official AAR blamed "faulty intelligence."

But Alex knew the truth. He had wanted to get the mission done. He wanted the efficiency metric green. He had ignored the gut feeling of his squad leader because the satellite data said the path was clear.

He had chosen data over judgment.

He looked at the second question on the form.

“What capability did you lose in that moment?”

Alex typed: Trust. And the ability to say no to a superior officer.

He stared at the words. It was the same feeling he had in Martin’s office. The pressure to conform to a script that felt wrong. The fear of saying "no" to an authority figure who claimed to know better.

A notification popped up on his screen. Incoming Transmission: Encrypted Channel.

It was Maya. Briefing in 1 hour. Bring your scars.

Alex closed the tablet. He looked at the empty coffee cup Elena had left behind.

He was a logistics expert. He knew that if you couldn't supply your own line, you couldn't hold the line. And right now, his supply line, his marriage, his family's trust, was stretching thin.

He stood up. He needed to get to The Bunker. He needed to find out why his failures were relevant to his bank account.

***

Location: The Bunker | 08:00 Hours

The Bunker was different today. The main screen was dark. The usual hum of servers was silenced, replaced by a low, rhythmic thumping sound.

Alex walked in. The lights were dimmed. In the center of the room, a single spotlight illuminated a chair.

JD sat in the chair. He wore a black turtleneck and a blazer. He looked like a priest conducting an exorcism. He held a thick file folder in his lap.

"Sit," JD said. His voice echoed slightly.

Alex sat on a crate opposite him.

Maya and Sanjay were in the shadows, watching. Neither of them spoke. Neither of them typed. The playfulness was gone. The atmosphere was thick with gravitas.

"You filled out the assessment," JD stated. It wasn't a question.

"Yes, sir."

"Let me guess," JD said, opening the folder. "You wrote about Kandahar. 2014. The convoy."

Alex stiffened. "How did you—"

"We have your file, Alex," JD said. "Not your military file. Your real file. Your psychological profile. Your fitness reports. Your therapy notes." He pulled out a sheet of paper. "Here it is. 'Officer displays high competence in execution but struggles with authority when presented with conflicting data. Tendency toward internalization of failure.'"

He looked up. "You blame yourself for Kandahar."

"I made the call," Alex said. "I followed the bad intel. I should have pushed back."

JD shook his head slowly. "No. That's not the lesson."

He tossed the paper onto the floor.

"The lesson," JD said, "is that you were operating on a Consumer Model of Risk. You were consuming the intelligence the Pentagon fed you. You trusted the supply chain of information."

JD stood up and walked to the whiteboard. He wrote: CONSUMER vs. COMMANDER.

"A consumer assumes the product is safe," JD said. "They assume the food in the grocery store isn't poisoned. They assume the label on the bottle is true. They consume the system."

He turned to Alex. "You were a consumer of intelligence. You didn't own the source. You didn't verify the terrain. You just... swallowed it."

"So, I was stupid," Alex said, his jaw tight.

"You were trained to be," Maya said from the shadows. Her voice was soft. "The military relies on the Consumer Model for the lower ranks. They need you to follow orders. They need you to trust the system. It's the only way, an army that big, functions."

"But" Sanjay added, stepping into the light, "you're not a lower rank anymore. You're a General in your own life now. And Generals don't consume intel. They manufacture it."

Alex looked at them. "What does this have to do with wealth?"

"Everything," JD said. He walked back to the chair and sat down. "Martin told you to buy the 'Glide Path.' Why?"

"Because the data says it works," Alex recited. "The Trinity Study. The four percent rule."

"You are consuming the data," JD said sharply. "You are trusting the supply chain. You are trusting that the people who manage the bond market have your best interests at heart. You are trusting that the currency won't collapse. You are trusting that inflation won't spike."

He leaned forward. "Alex, look at the economic terrain of the last five years. Is it stable?"

“No.”

“Then why are you consuming a strategy designed for a stable world?”

Alex felt the cold realization seeping into his bones. He was doing it again. He was sitting in the Humvee, looking at the satellite map that said "clear," while his gut told him there were IEDs buried in the road.

“So, what’s the alternative?” Alex asked. “How do I stop consuming?”

“You start with a Debrief,” JD said. “Not of your successes. Of your failures. Because your failures contain your edge.”

JD tapped the folder. “I want to tell you a story about a failure. My failure.”

Alex sat up straighter. JD never talked about his past.

“It was 1993,” JD said, his voice low. “Mogadishu. Black Hawk Down. I was a Lt. Colonel then. I was in the TOC (Tactical Operations Center). We had the best technology in the world. We had satellites. We had night vision. We had the most lethal fighting force on the planet.”

He paused. “And we got our asses kicked by a bunch of teenagers with AK-47s and technicals.”

“Because of the terrain,” Alex said. “The city. The alleyways. The chaos.”

"Because of the asymmetry," JD corrected. "We were trying to fight a linear war in a non-linear environment. We were bringing a tank to a knife fight in a phone booth."

He looked at Alex. "The financial world is Mogadishu right now. It's a non-linear environment. It's chaos. Algorithms trading against algorithms. Crypto crashing and soaring in hours. Supply chains breaking overnight."

"And Martin is trying to fight it with a tank," Alex said.

"Exactly," JD said. "He's trying to use a 1990s strategy in a 2030 war. He's driving a Humvee through the alleyways."

JD stood up and walked to the dark screen. He snapped his fingers.

The screen lit up.

It wasn't a map. It was a video. A dashcam video.

"This was taken three days ago," JD said. "In Long Beach, California."

The video showed a chaotic scene at a shipping port. Cranes were idle. Containers were stacked high. Dozens of trucks were idling, engines roaring, drivers screaming.

"What am I looking at?" Alex asked.

"A gridlock," Maya said. "A logistical failure. A shipping company called 'Ocean Star' went bankrupt. Their creditors seized the assets. They locked the gates. Thousands of containers are sitting there. Perishables rotting. Electronics rusting."

"And?" Alex asked. "It's sad. But what's the opportunity?"

"Look closer," JD said.

He zoomed in on one of the containers. It was stenciled with a logo: Aether Dynamics.

Alex froze. He knew that name. Aether Dynamics made the guidance chips for the JDAM missiles he used to order. They were high-tech, low-supply, critical infrastructure.

"Aether didn't go bankrupt," Alex said, thinking out loud. "They're a victim. Their supply chain is cut off."

"Precisely," JD said. "They have a quarterly shipment of chips stuck in that container. They need those chips to fulfill a defense contract. If they don't deliver, they default. And if they default..."

"Their stock tanks," Alex finished.

"Their stock tanks," JD agreed. "And the vultures circle."

Sanjay stepped forward. "I've been tracking their stock. It's down 15% this week. The narrative is 'Supply Chain Issues.' The rumor is 'Insolvency.'"

"But it's not insolvency," Alex said. "It's a liquidity trap."

"Bingo," Sanjay said. "It's a liquidity trap. Aether is healthy. They just can't get their product."

JD turned to Alex. The spotlight reflected in his eyes. "This is the Debrief, Alex. This is why we analyzed your failure in

Kandahar. You failed because you relied on the system's logistics. You waited for the convoy."

He pointed at the screen. "Aether is waiting for the convoy. They are sitting there like ducks in a shooting gallery, waiting for the bankruptcy court to release their own goods."

"So, what's the play?" Alex asked. "Buy the stock?"

"Too passive," Maya said. "That's consumer thinking. 'Buy low, sell high.' Boring."

"Commander thinking," JD said, "is solving the problem. You have the resources, Alex. You have the contacts. You know how logistics works. You know the Port Authority captains. You know the union bosses."

Alex stared at the screen. The chaos. The screaming drivers. The idle cranes.

He felt a familiar itch in his fingertips. The itch to give an order. To clear the fog. To make the machine move.

"You want me to go to Long Beach," Alex said. "You want me to unblock the port."

"I want you to command the port," JD corrected. "I want you to go down there, cut through the red tape, negotiate with the creditors, and get that container to Aether."

"And what do I get out of it?" Alex asked. It wasn't about greed. It was about the deal.

"Equity," Sanjay said. "We've already structured a deal with Aether's CFO. They are desperate. If you can deliver that container in 72 hours, they will give us preferred stock. warrants. A massive equity stake. Not at market price. At the distressed price."

"A private bailout," Alex said. "A sovereign intervention."

"By you," JD said. "Your First Command."

Alex watched the video loop. The chaos. The noise. It looked exactly like the briefing room in Kandahar. Conflicting data. No clear path.

But this time, he wasn't the Major waiting for orders. He was the Commander.

He knew the terrain. He knew the players. He spoke the language of logistics. This wasn't finance. This was warfare.

He looked at JD. He looked at Maya. He looked at Sanjay.

They weren't asking him to trust a computer model. They were asking him to trust himself.

"Book the flight," Alex said.

"Already done," Maya said, smiling. The tablet in her hand lit up green. "You leave at 0600 tomorrow. Sanjay is going with you."

Sanjay grinned. "I've never seen a riot before. I brought my GoPro."

Alex looked back at the screen. The gridlock.

He was going to war again.

Not against terrorists. Not against nations.

But against inefficiency. Against the friction that stopped the world from turning.

And he was going to win.

***

Lesson Learnt:

- Military Doctrine: The Intelligence Failure. Passive consumption of data leads to disaster. A Commander must own the intelligence cycle. They must verify the terrain with their own eyes. History is not just a record of events; it is a database of "what not to do."

- Financial Doctrine: Private Sovereign Intervention. Most investors look at the market and ask, "What will happen?" The Commander looks at a problem and asks, "Can I solve it?" Wealth is not just buying assets; it is creating value by solving logistical bottlenecks, that institutions are too bureaucratic to fix. This is "Private Equity" on a personal scale, using your specific, high-level skills to unlock value that is invisible to the generic investor.

Chapter 4: The Three-Theater War

Location: Long Beach, California | The Port of Entry | 13:00 Hours

The heat in Long Beach didn't just sit on your skin; it tasted like diesel. It was a thick, oily soup of exhaust, salt air, and rotting fruit.

Alex Rivera stood on the roof of their rental car parked on a block, overlooking the Port of Los Angeles. He wore a blazer over a tactical t-shirt, holding a pair of binoculars. He looked like a plainclothes cop who had swapped coffee for pure adrenaline.

"It looks like a parking lot for giants," Sanjay Mehta said, leaning against the car door. He was eating a churro, sugar dusting his beard. "Except the giants are robots and they're on strike."

Below them, the port was paralyzed. Thousands of container ships, some, the size of the Chrysler Building, sat anchored in the harbor, their lights twinkling in the midday smog. The cranes on the dock stood motionless, their long arms hanging limp like dead insects.

"The strike is a cover," Alex said, lowering the binoculars. "Look at the security perimeter."

He pointed to the fence line. Private security in black SUVs were patrolling the gap between the Union picket line and the terminal gates.

"Creditors?" Sanjay asked, licking sugar off his thumb.

"Mercenaries," Alex corrected. "Aether Dynamics' creditors didn't just seize the assets. They hired a private security firm to lockdown the terminal. They're trying to starve Aether out."

"Why?"

"Because if Aether defaults on the debt, the creditors get the intellectual property," Alex said, checking his watch. "They don't care about the chips. They care about the patents. This isn't a logistics dispute. It's a hostile takeover."

Sanjay whistled. "So, we're walking into a corporate war zone. Cool. I'm wearing my good shoes."

Alex ignored him. He was thinking about the briefing he'd received on the flight over. JD had sent him a tactical map of his finances; overlaid with the concept they called The Three-Theater War.

It had blown his mind.

For twenty-six years, the military had taught Alex to fight on a single, integrated battlefield. But in wealth, the experts were giving terrible advice because they didn't understand the doctrine of theaters.

"Martin says to diversify," Alex muttered, more to himself than to Sanjay. "He says spread your money out. But that's like deploying an infantry division to the Arctic, a tank division to the jungle, and an air wing to the middle of the ocean. You're not diversifying. You're diluting your force."

Sanjay looked at him. "English, Commander. I speak three languages, but 'Military Grumble' isn't one of them."

Alex turned to him. "Sanjay, imagine you have a tank. You don't take it into a swamp. You don't take it into a city center. You take it to the desert where it can maneuver."

"Okay."

"Most people," Alex said, gesturing to the chaotic port below, "put their tank in the swamp. They treat their retirement money the same way they treat their gambling money. They use the same strategy for their 'Home Theater', their safety, their mortgage, their kids' education, as they do for their 'Expeditionary Theater', their high-risk bets."

"And that's bad?"

"It's suicide," Alex said. "Because when the Expeditionary Theater gets hit, and it always gets hit, you lose the tank. And since you parked it right next to the mess hall, you starve."

He pulled out his tablet. The screen displayed a schematic of three distinct zones.

THEATER 1: HOME TERRITORY (The Defense) Mission: Survival. Security. Non-negotiable obligations. Doctrine: Fortification. Impenetrable defenses. Zero risk. Asset: Home equity (properly managed), emergency reserves, guaranteed income streams.

THEATER 2: EXPEDITIONARY FORCE (The Offense) Mission: Conquest. High growth. Wealth acceleration. Doctrine: Asymmetric warfare. High risk, high reward. "Send the special ops, not the supply clerks." Asset: Private equity, angel investing, crypto, high-volatility stocks.

THEATER 3: THE LEGACY (The Diplomatic Corps) Mission: Influence. Multi-generational continuity. Doctrine: Strategic patience. Infrastructure that outlives the commander. Asset: Trusts, foundations, education endowments, art/collectibles, political capital.

"The mistake everyone makes," Alex said, tapping the screen, "is keeping their Home Theater money in the Expeditionary zone. They invest their rent money in the stock market. That's why they panic when the market drops. They aren't panic-selling a stock; they're panic-selling the roof over their head."

He looked at the port. "We are about to enter the Expeditionary Theater, Sanjay. We are going to break that blockade. But we are not risking the Home Theater to do it. If this goes south, Elena's house, your parents' retirement, none of that is touched. We are using allocated capital. Capital we can afford to lose but hope to multiply."

Sanjay finished his churro. "So, we're not betting the farm. We're betting a cow?"

"We're betting a calf," Alex said. "To win a herd."

He threw the binoculars to Sanjay. "Let's move. JD's contact at Aether is waiting at the security gate. We have a window of twenty minutes before the shift change."

***

Location: Gate 4, Long Beach Terminal | 14:15 Hours

The heat was shimmering off the asphalt. The air smelled of sulfur and ozone. A line of semi-trucks was idling outside the gate, engines growling, exhaust fuming. The drivers stood outside, leaning against their trucks, smoking cigarettes and looking angry.

Alex and Sanjay walked past the trucks. They were underdressed for the industrial grit, overdressed for the union protest. They stuck out like two FBI agents at a biker rally.

At the gate, a man in a hard hat and a yellow safety vest stood next to a boom barrier. He had a clipboard in one hand and a face that said he hated everyone he met.

“Gate’s closed,” the man shouted before they were even close. “Back of the line.”

Alex kept walking. He didn't break stride.

“I said, back of the—”

Alex stopped three feet from the man. He didn't smile. He didn't speak. He simply engaged his Command Presence.

It was a technique JD had taught him years ago. You don't yell. You don't threaten. You just project the absolute certainty that you belong here, and that any obstacle you encounter is a clerical error by the universe that you are about to correct.

The man looked at Alex. He saw the eyes. Cold, flat, unblinking. He saw the posture. Shoulders squared. Hands visible but ready.

Then he looked at Sanjay, who was grinning like a kid at a carnival.

“Uh,” the guard said. “Who are you?”

“Logistics Consultancy for the receivership,” Alex said. He used a term he’d made up two minutes ago, but he said it with the authority of a Supreme Court Justice. “Here to verify the manifest on Container 4-Alpha-9.”

The guard frowned. He looked down at his clipboard. “Nobody told me about a consult.”

"We don't report to the gate," Alex said quietly. "We report to the bondholders. The bondholders report to the courts. The courts report to the laws. Where do you report to, Sergeant?"

The guard bristled. "I am not a Sergeant. I'm a Teamster."

Alex softened his expression. A fraction of an inch. Just enough to signal mutual respect. "My apologies, brother. Just a figure of speech. Look, we're just here to check the seal. We'll be in and out in ten minutes. You stay here, we go in, nobody knows we were gone. You keep your line secure."

The guard hesitated. He looked at the angry truck drivers. He looked at the private security SUVs parked nearby. He looked at Alex, who radiated the kind of calm competence that people naturally followed.

"Hurry up," the guard said, lifting the boom barrier. "And don't touch anything."

"Understood," Alex said.

They walked through the gate and into the maze of containers.

***

Location: Inside the Terminal | 14:30 Hours

The scale of the terminal was disorienting. The containers stacked ten stories high created canyons of steel, blocking the sun. It was a city built for machines, not humans.

Sanjay was walking backwards, filming with his phone. "This is epic. It's like a level in Fallout."

"Focus, Sanjay," Alex said, checking the GPS on his tablet. "Target is three blocks east."

They turned a corner and found it. Container 4-Alpha-9.

It was painted in faded blue. On the side, stenciled in yellow letters: AETHER DYNAMICS - CLASSIFIED MILITARY CIRCUITRY.

It looked innocent. Just a steel box. But Alex knew that inside that box was millions of dollars of technology, and the future of a company that the creditors were trying to bleed dry.

"Okay," Alex said, stopping a few yards away. "Now for the hard part."

He pulled out a satellite phone. He dialed a number JD had given him.

"Brennan," a voice answered.

"Mr. Brennan," Alex said. "This is Rivera. I'm looking at the package."

"Good," Brennan said. The voice was smooth. Too smooth. "Did you bring the release order from the court?"

Alex paused. This was the test.

"No," Alex said. "The court order is stalled in the system. You know that. You paid the right people to stall it."

There was silence on the line.

“I’m not here with a lawyer,” Alex continued. “I’m here with a mechanic. I can release the goods right now. But I need a guarantee from Aether that they will honor the warrant contract we discussed.”

Brennan laughed. A dry, humorless sound. “You and what army, Rivera? You think you can just walk out of here with that container?”

“I don’t need an army,” Alex said. “I need leverage.”

He signaled to Sanjay. Sanjay nodded and tapped a command on his tablet.

Suddenly, a siren began to wail inside the terminal. It wasn't a loud, blaring alarm. It was the deep, rhythmic horn of the cranes.

“What is that?” Brennan asked, his voice tightening.

“Sanjay just accessed the terminal’s operating system,” Alex said. “Maya found a backdoor. It wasn't hard; the security software is three years out of date.”

“Stop it!” Brennan shouted.

“I can’t,” Alex lied. “The system is initiating a safety lockdown. All cranes are going to go into emergency mode in five minutes. When they do, they’ll automatically discharge their loads.”

“You’ll destroy the containers!”

"Not all of them," Alex said. "Just the ones over the side of the dock. Including yours, Mr. Brennan. You're parked right on Pier B."

Alex checked the map. Brennan's office was indeed in the danger zone. The creditors had set up shop right in the blast radius.

"You're bluffing," Brennan said.

"Am I?" Alex said. "Look out of your window."

The sounds of chaos were starting. Forklifts were honking. Security guards were running.

"Here is the deal," Alex said, his voice dropping into a register that terrified junior officers. "You authorize the release of this container to my custody. You call your goons at the gate and tell them to let us leave. In exchange, Sanjay here aborts the crash sequence. You get your bonds. We get our chips. Everyone goes home happy."

"You're a lunatic," Brennan said.

"I'm a Commander," Alex corrected. "And I have seized the high ground. You have thirty seconds."

Silence on the line. Alex watched the second hand on his watch.

Twenty-eight.

Twenty-nine.

"Fine!" Brennan shouted. "Take it! Tell your hacker to stand down!"

"Done," Alex said. He signaled Sanjay. The siren cut off abruptly.

The silence that followed was louder than the noise.

Alex hung up the phone. He looked at the container.

"Sanjay, call the truck."

Sanjay was staring at him, eyes wide. "That was the most illegal thing I've ever done."

"It wasn't illegal," Alex said. "It was asymmetric warfare. We used their own fear against them. Sun Tzu would be proud."

He put a hand on the side of the container. The metal was hot.

"But the real lesson," Alex said, looking up at the towering steel, "is Theaters."

"What do you mean?"

"If we had lost," Alex said, "If Brennan hadn't blinked, what would have happened?"

Sanjay shrugged. "We would have run away. Gotten arrested. Probably sued."

"Exactly," Alex said. "And that would have been fine. Because we didn't bet the House on this. We didn't bet Elena's future. We bet a plane ticket, a rental car, and a few hours of legal risk. That's the Expeditionary Theater. You risk a division to take a hill. You don't risk the capital."

He looked at the shipping container. "This is our hill. And we just took it."

The truck arrived. A massive diesel beast. The driver looked confused, but he didn't ask questions when Sanjay handed him a wad of cash.

As the crane lifted the container onto the flatbed, Alex walked to the edge of the pier. He looked out at the ocean.

He felt it. The shift.

For years, he had been the one guarding the perimeter. He had been the one saluting the officers, following the orders.

Now, he was the one giving the orders. He was the one manipulating the variables. He was the one creating the leverage.

He took out his phone. He dialed Elena.

It rang three times.

"Hey," she said. She sounded busy. Typing in the background.

"Hey," Alex said. "I'm in California."

"California?" She stopped typing. "Why? The flight said you were going to—"

"Just business," he said. "I wanted to check in. How's... everything?"

"Everything is fine," she said slowly. "Alex, what's going on? You're acting strange."

Alex watched the container being strapped down. The deal was done. The equity was secured. The Wealth Command OS had just executed its first successful subroutine.

"I'm not acting strange, Elena," Alex said, his voice steady. "I'm just changing my operating system."

"What does that mean?"

"It means," he said, looking at the horizon, "that I'm done apologizing for being good at what I do."

He paused.

"I'm coming home tomorrow. And when I do, I want to sit down with you. I want to show you something. A plan. Not for retirement. For command."

Silence on the line. Then, a soft exhale.

"Okay, Alex," she said. "But it better be a good plan."

Alex smiled. A real smile. The first one in months.

"It's a war plan, Elena," he said. "And we're going to win."

He hung up.

Sanjay walked over, panting from exertion. "Truck is rolling. Brennan is screaming at his lawyers. The Union guys are clapping. It's a party."

"Good," Alex said. "Let's get to the airport."

They walked back toward the gate, past the angry trucks, past the confused guards. They walked through the chaos like they owned the place.

And for the first time, Alex realized, he did.

***

Lesson Learnt:

- Military Doctrine: Theater Command. A General does not command a single battle; he commands a theater of operations. He allocates resources between defense, offense, and supply lines based on the strategic objective. You cannot use the same tactics for a fortress defense (Home) that you use for a raiding party (Expeditionary).

- Financial Doctrine: The Three-Theater Wealth System.

    1. Home Theater (The Fortress): Assets must be protected with zero tolerance for loss. This is your psychological safety net. If you gamble this money, you lose the ability to take risks elsewhere.

    2. Expeditionary Theater (The Raid): Allocated capital designed for high risk. You expect volatility here. You don't panic when it drops; you exploit it. This is your growth engine.

3. Legacy Theater (The Empire): Strategic assets built for the long term, immune to short-term market noise.

The Insight: Most investors lose because they fight a "Two-Theater War" on a single battlefield, mixing their defensive capital with their offensive bets. The Commander separates them. He fortifies his home, deploys his expedition, and ignores the market noise that scares the civilians.

Chapter 5: Intelligence Failure

Location: The Rivera Residence | Living Room | Saturday, 09:00 Hours

The noise didn't have a physical form, but it felt like a weight.

Alex sat on his living room sofa, a cup of coffee balanced on his knee, staring at the television. The volume was low, but the aggression was high.

On the screen, a man in a shiny blue suit was screaming. He wasn't angry; he was excited. He was waving a red marker at a chart that looked like a seismograph recording an earthquake.

"THIS IS THE DIP!" the man screamed. "THIS IS THE BUY SIGNAL! IF YOU DON'T GET IN NOW, YOU'RE GOING TO WATCH THE ROCKET SHIP LEAVE WITHOUT YOU!"

Alex looked at the bottom of the screen. The ticker tape was scrolling faster than the human eye could read, a blur of green and red arrows, acronyms, and numbers.

GE -1.2% TSLA +4.5% AMZN -0.8% GOLD +0.2% OIL -1.1%

It was visual chaos. It was a hallucination in data form.

On the coffee table, Elena's phone vibrated. Then it dinged. Then it vibrated again.

She walked into the room, carrying a basket of laundry. She looked tired. The "Weekend Warrior" fatigue of the suburban upper-middle class.

"Did you hear?" she asked, tossing a sock onto the pile. "The Fed Chair is speaking at Jackson Hole next week. The guys on the radio are saying interest rates are going to double."

Alex looked at the TV. The man in the blue suit was now interviewing a "Chief Economist" from a bank Alex had never heard of.

"The economy is resilient!" the economist shouted over the blue suit. "Inflation is transitory! The consumer is strong! BUY THE DIP!"

Alex felt a headache starting behind his eyes. It was the same feeling he used to get in the Tactical Operations Center when two different intelligence agencies were feeding him conflicting reports. One said the village was friendly. The other said there was a sniper on the mosque.

Conflict. Contradiction. Noise.

"Which is it, Elena?" Alex asked, gesturing to the screen with his coffee cup. "Are we doomed, or are we about to get rich?"

Elena sighed, sitting down and picking up her phone. She unlocked it, swiped through a news app. "Well, the Times says we're heading for a recession because of the housing market."

She opened another app. "But Bloomberg says tech stocks are going to the moon because of AI."

She opened a third. "And my crypto group says fiat currency is dead, and we should all buy llama-themed coins."

She looked at Alex, her eyes wide with that specific brand of modern anxiety. "I don't know, Alex. I feel like everyone is shouting, and no one is saying anything."

Alex put the coffee cup down. He thought about the Long Beach port. About the container. About the calm certainty of JD's voice.

"The first casualty of war is truth."

But in the financial world, truth wasn't the casualty. Attention was the casualty. The media, the apps, the pundits, they weren't fighting for the truth. They were fighting for his eyeballs.

"It's an Intelligence Failure," Alex said quietly.

"What?"

"A systemic intelligence failure," Alex said, his voice dropping into the lecture cadence. "In the military, if you have bad intel, people die. If you have too much intel, you get paralyzed. And if you have conflicting intel, you make the wrong move."

He pointed to the TV. "That man? The blue suit? He's selling urgency. He wants you to panic-buy or panic-sell because panic generates volume. And volume generates fees."

He pointed to Elena's phone. "And those apps? They're selling anxiety. They want you to click because clicks generate ad revenue."

Elena looked at her phone. "But... how am I supposed to know what to do? We have the college fund. We have the mortgage."

"You are drowning in data, Elena," Alex said. "But you are starving for intelligence."

He stood up and walked over to the television. He pressed the power button. The shouting man vanished. The ticker tape disappeared. The room went silent.

The silence felt heavy for a second, like the air pressure dropping before a storm. Then, it felt peaceful.

Alex turned back to his wife.

"Martin sends you these reports," Alex said. "The pie charts. The 'Glide Path.' He thinks he's giving you intelligence. But he's just giving you a map of a terrain that changed three months ago."

Elena bit her lip. "So, what do we do? We can't just ignore the world."

"No," Alex said, checking his watch. He had a briefing at The Bunker in an hour. "We don't ignore the world. We filter it. We need to separate the Signal from the Noise."

He walked over and kissed her on the forehead. "Go, do the laundry. I'm going to find out what's actually happening."

***

Location: The Bunker | The Black Room | 10:30 Hours

The Bunker was darker than usual. Maya had taped blackout plastic over the small windows near the ceiling. The air conditioning was humming aggressively.

Sanjay sat in the center of the room on a yoga ball, bouncing gently, staring at a wall of monitors that displayed nothing but raw code. JD stood in the corner, sharpening a pocketknife with a slow, rhythmic shhh-shhh sound.

"Welcome to the Black Room," Maya said. She was wearing a hoodie today, the hood up, her face illuminated by the glow of three different screens. "This is where we kill the noise."

Alex walked in. The atmosphere was different. It felt like a submarine, submerged deep beneath the turbulent waves of the market.

"I just watched CNBC at home," Alex said, pulling up a stool. "I think my IQ dropped ten points."

"That's the point," Sanjay said, stopping his bouncing. "CNBC isn't news. It's entertainment for people who hate their money. It's financial porn."

JD looked up from his knife. "Tell him, Alex. What is the difference between Data, Information, and Intelligence?"

Alex leaned forward. He knew this. It was Intelligence 101.

"Data is raw," Alex said. "It's numbers. It's stock prices. It's the temperature outside."

"Information is data with context," Alex continued. "It's a stock price drop of 5% combined with the news that their CEO quit. It connects the dots."

"And Intelligence?" JD asked, his eyes narrowing.

"Intelligence is analysis," Alex said, feeling the old commander's mindset click into place. "It's understanding why the CEO quit. It's predicting who the next CEO will be. It's knowing that the 5% drop is a buying opportunity because the company is sound, or a selling signal because the CEO was embezzling funds. Intelligence is the ability to predict the future based on the hidden variables."

JD pointed the knife at him. "Correct. And the financial industry is designed to keep you stuck at the Data level."

He walked to the main console and typed a command. The screens changed. They were no longer showing code. They were showing news headlines from every major outlet in the world, laid out in a grid.

CNN, FOX, BBC, REUTERS, BLOOMBERG, AL JAZEERA, ZERO HEDGE.

"Look at this," JD said. "The Global Narrative. It looks like chaos. But look for the repetition."

He pointed to a cluster of headlines.

"INFLATION FEARS RISE AS OIL PRICES CLIMB" "CONSUMERS FEEL PINCH AT THE PUMP" "FED WATCHERS PREDICT AGGRESSIVE RATE HIKES"

"Same story," Alex said. "Different fonts."

"Exactly," Maya said. "This is the Narrative Injection. The large institutions, the hedge funds, the banks, pay PR firms to plant these stories. They seed the narrative."

"Why?" Alex asked. "Why pay for a story about oil prices?"

Sanjay laughed. "Because they want to 'short' the oil sector. They bet billions that oil stocks would go down. Now, they need the herd to panic-sell oil stocks so they can buy them back at the bottom to cover their short. It's a classic False Flag Operation."

Alex stared at the screen. He thought of the blue-suited man on TV screaming about inflation. He wasn't reporting news; he was acting as a mercenary for a hedge fund. He was a psy-ops operative.

"So, the retail investor," Alex said slowly, "is the insurgent getting targeted by propaganda."

"And you're losing the war," JD said. "Because your brain isn't wired to handle this amount of data. You're trying to process a terabyte of information every minute. You freeze. You make emotional decisions. You sell when you should buy. You buy when you should sell."

He pulled a red cloth out of his pocket and tossed it over the screen.

"Today," JD said, "we learn how to go Dark. We learn how to build a listening post that doesn't listen to the shouting masses."

Maya typed furiously. The screen under the red cloth changed. When she pulled it back, the headlines were gone. Replaced by a single, black map of the world.

There were blinking white dots on the map. Not over cities. Over oceans and ports.

"What am I looking at?" Alex asked.

"Commercial shipping traffic," Maya said. "Satellite telemetry. We aren't looking at the news, Alex. We're looking at the physical reality of the economy."

She pointed to a dot in the Indian Ocean. "That's a cargo ship carrying iron ore from Brazil to China. It's been sitting idle for four days."

"So?" Sanjay asked. "Engine trouble?"

"No engine trouble," Maya said. "It's full. But the receiving port in Qingdao is gridlocked. They can't unload."

"Okay," Alex said, trying to connect the dots. "So, the iron ore is stuck in the water. What does that mean?"

"It means," Maya said, zooming in on a different map, a map of steel futures prices, "that the steel supply chain in China is about to take a hit. And when Chinese steel supply drops, global construction costs spike. And when construction costs spike, certain stocks get hammered."

She looked at Alex. "The news hasn't reported this yet. The port authority in China is trying to keep it quiet. But the satellites don't lie."

Alex felt the thrill. The cold, electric rush of knowing something the enemy didn't.

This was Asymmetric Intelligence.

The institutions had their own satellites, sure. But they also had bureaucracy. They had committees. By the time the data moved from the satellite to the analyst, to the trader, to the portfolio manager, the window had closed.

The Bunker had Maya, Sanjay, and Alex. They were a Special Ops team.

"When does the news hit?" Alex asked.

Maya checked her watch. "Three days. Maybe four."

"And what do we do?"

"We don't wait for the news," JD said. "We move now. We short the construction sector in the Asian markets. We buy the shipping insurance companies who will see a spike in claims due to the delay."

"But if the news doesn't come out?" Alex asked. "If they fix the port?"

"Then we exit the trade with a small loss," JD said, shrugging. "That's war. You win some, you lose some. But you play the odds when the odds are in your favor. The information asymmetry is your advantage."

Alex looked at the blinking light on the screen.

He realized that for years, he had been a passive consumer of information. He had been a civilian standing in the town square, listening to the latest gossip. He had been reacting.

Commanders don't react. Commanders initiate.

"I'm ready for the exercise," Alex said.

Sanjay clapped his hands together. "Oh boy! The Game. I love the Game."

***

Location: The Bunker - The Simulation Deck | 11:00 Hours

Maya cleared a whiteboard. She wrote a single word in the center.

LEADERSHIP.

“Okay, Alex,” she said. “Here is the scenario. You have $50,000 in your ‘Expeditionary Fund.’ We are going to simulate a news cycle.”

She handed him a headset. “Put these on. Noises off.”

Alex put the headset on. The world went silent.

Sanjay sat at a computer, acting as the "Market Maker." Maya acted as the "News Feed."

“Game start,” Maya said.

A screen in front of Alex flashed. “BREAKING: CEO OF TECH GIANT ‘NEXUS’ RESIGNS AMID SEXUAL HARASSMENT ALLEGATIONS.” “STOCK: NXS - PRE-MARKET DROPPING 15%.”

Alex stared at the screen. It was visceral. The red numbers. The sensational headline.

His instinct was immediate. Sell. Sell everything. Get out before it hits zero. It’s radioactive.

He looked at his keyboard. His finger hovered over the ‘SELL’ button.

“Wait,” he whispered to himself.

He remembered the "Listening Post." He looked to his left, where a second screen showed the Dark Data.

It showed the volume of options trades on NXS. While the stock was plummeting in pre-market, someone was buying massive amounts of Call Options. Bets that the stock would go up.

"Who would buy calls on a burning building?" Alex muttered.

He looked at the timeline. The allegations were anonymous. No proof. Just a rumor.

This was a False Flag. Someone wanted the stock to drop. A hedge fund was likely shorting the stock, planting the rumor, and planning to buy back the cheap shares.

This was an Indignation Attack.

The market was ruled by emotion, not math. Right now, the emotion was outrage. But the math, the dark flow of money, was showing accumulation.

Alex smiled. He pressed 'BUY.'

He used all $50,000 to buy shares of the plummeting company.

The screen flashed red. His account value dropped immediately to $42,000. The red numbers pulsed like a wound.

"Alex, are you sure?" Maya asked, her voice neutral. "The news is reporting more allegations. The stock is down 20% now."

"I know," Alex said, staring at the options volume. "I'm betting the rumors are fake. I'm betting the algorithm is bluffing."

"Wait," Sanjay said, his voice crackling over the headset. "The volume just spiked. An institutional buyer is stepping in."

The red line on the chart stumbled. It hit bottom. Then, it bounced.

The Dead Cat Bounce? No, it was stronger.

Suddenly, a new headline flashed across the top of Maya's feed. "CEO OF NEXUS DENIES ALLEGATIONS, RELEASES EMAIL PROVING ALIBI. ALLEGED VICTIM CONFESSED TO BEING PAID BY SHORT SELLER."

The stock line went vertical. It shot up like a missile.

Alex watched his account value climb. $45,000. $50,000. $60,000. $75,000.

He had turned $50,000 into $75,000 in ten minutes.

"Stop," Alex said, hitting the sell button as the momentum peaked. He sold at the top.

His account settled at $72,000.

He pulled off the headset. The room was quiet.

Maya was looking at her monitors. Sanjay was whistling. JD stood by the whiteboard, a faint smile on his face.

"Twenty-two thousand dollars profit," JD said. "Ten minutes. Tell me how you did it."

"I ignored the news," Alex said, his adrenaline still spiking. "The news was the noise. It was the deception. I trusted the flow."

"The dark data," JD said. "The institutional money. They don't buy on rumors. They buy on truth."

He walked over to Alex and put a hand on his shoulder.

"Welcome to the Intelligence Gap, Alex. That is the gap where wealth lives. The gap between what the public thinks is happening, and what the insiders know is happening."

Alex looked at the screen. The profit was tangible. But the feeling was better.

He hadn't guessed. He hadn't been lucky. He had read the terrain. He had identified the enemy's deception.

He thought about the people at home, watching the blue-suited man scream about NXs. They had sold at the bottom. They had locked in their losses. They were angry, scared, and poorer.

And here, in the dark, cool air of The Bunker, Alex was richer, calmer, and in control.

"Martin," Alex said. "My financial advisor."

"What about him?" Sanjay asked.

"He sends me these newsletters," Alex said. "He calls me with 'tips.' I realized today... he's just reading the news. He's just a consumer of the propaganda. He's not the source. He's a repeater."

"Exactly," JD said. "He is a logistics officer counting rations. He doesn't know what the enemy is doing."

JD walked to the blackout curtain and pulled it back a fraction. A sliver of sunlight pierced the gloom, illuminating dust motes dancing in the air.

"The world is loud, Alex," JD said. "It's screaming for your attention. It's trying to make you afraid, so you'll pay for protection. It's trying to make you greedy, so you'll pay for access."

He looked at the map of the shipping container, still blinking on the dark screen.

"But real intelligence is quiet," JD said. "It's the hum of the servers. It's the movement of a ship on the ocean. It's the silence before the shot."

Alex stood up. He felt the weight of his phone in his pocket. He knew that when he walked out of here, the noise would try to reclaim him. The news apps. The gossip. The fear.

But he had the filter now.

He had the OS.

He had the Command.

“I’m going home,” Alex said. “I need to tell Elena about the ‘Intelligence Gap.’”

“Good luck,” Maya said, not looking up from her screen. “She’s probably watching Jim Cramer right now.”

Alex paused. “Then I have some deprogramming to do.”

He walked to the door, leaving the silence of The Bunker behind. He was stepping back into the noise, but for the first time, he wasn't afraid of the sound.

He was conducting the orchestra.

***

Lesson Learnt:

- Military Doctrine: Intelligence vs. Noise. A Commander must ruthlessly filter information. Public reports are often outdated or manipulated (Deception). Reliable intelligence comes from direct observation, listening posts, and trusted sources, not the rumor mill.

- Financial Doctrine: The Narrative Injection & The Dark Data. Financial news is often created by market participants to manipulate price (Short sellers planting rumors). By ignoring the "public narrative" and focusing on "dark data" (institutional flows, supply chain logistics, alternative data), an investor gains an Asymmetric Advantage. You play the game the institutions play, not the game the TV tells you to play. Wealth is built in the silence between the headlines.

Part II: The Operating System

(Building the Weapon)

Chapter 6: Know Yourself, Know Your Wealth

Location: The Willow Creek Country Club | 14:00 Hours

The grass at Willow Creek was the kind of green that didn't exist in nature. It was chemically engineered perfection, the botanical equivalent of a botoxed smile. It stretched out toward the horizon, interrupted only by sand traps that looked less like hazards and more like carefully raked Zen gardens.

Alex Rivera stood on the patio of the clubhouse, holding a glass of iced tea that was ninety percent sugar and ten percent tea. Around him, the "Old Guard" of the defense contracting world mingled.

They were the survivors. The ones who had retired five, ten years ago. They had the tans, the relaxed shoulders, and the soft bellies of men who had stopped fighting gravity years ago.

"Alex! Good to see you, son!"

It was Bob Henderson. He wore a salmon-colored polo shirt that screamed "I have given up." Bob was a retired Lieutenant Colonel who now sells insurance to other retirees. It was a pyramid scheme of caution.

"Good to see you, Bob," Alex said, gripping Bob's hand. It was soft, like a damp sponge.

"Enjoying the freedom?" Bob asked, winking. "No more 0400 wake-up calls. No more Congressional hearings. Just the sweet life, right?"

Alex looked out over the golf course. A group of retirees were chipping onto the ninth green. They moved slowly. Deliberately. Like they were trying not to disturb the air.

"It's... quiet," Alex said.

"That's the point!" Bob laughed, clapping him on the shoulder. "Quiet is good. Quiet is safe. You know, I've got a little cottage in the Outer Banks. Just bought it. Going to sit on the porch and watch the waves. Maybe catch some fish."

"Sounds nice," Alex said, trying to inject enthusiasm into his voice.

"You should think about it," Bob said. "You've got the pension. You've got the time. You don't want to be one of those guys who keeps working until he drops dead. The

'Warrior Monks'. Sad, really. They don't know when to put the sword down."

Alex took a sip of the syrupy tea. The sweetness cloyed in his throat.

"The sword," Alex said, looking at the distant flagpole. "Sometimes I worry that if I put it down, I'll forget how to pick it up again."

Bob frowned. The comment had disrupted the Zen of the afternoon. "Alex, you're thinking too much. That's the military brain. You need to rewire. You need to... downsize your ambition. Upsize your relaxation."

Bob gestured to the sprawling clubhouse. "Look around you. We have everything we need. We play golf. We play bridge. We gossip. It's the peace dividend."

Alex looked at the crowd. He saw the vacancy behind their eyes. They weren't at peace; they were paused. Like a DVD left on pause for so long the screen had burned the image into the glass.

They were safe. They were comfortable. They were boring.

And they were all slowly dying.

"I'll think about it, Bob," Alex said.

"Do that," Bob said, moving on to his next victim. "Oh, hey! Is that Frank? Frank, you old dog!"

Alex stood alone by the railing. He watched a foursome tee off. They swung their clubs with the rhythm of metronomes. Predictable. Safe.

He felt a sudden, violent itch in his fingers. He wanted a weapon. He wanted a map. He wanted a problem that required a solution, not a golf swing that required a handicap.

He felt, Bob was so wrong. The problem wasn't that he couldn't put the sword down. The problem was that the sword was the only thing that made him feel real.

He wasn't a golfer. He wasn't a fisherman. He was a Commander.

And a Commander without a command is just a man with a lot of guns and no bullets.

***

Location: The Bunker | The Kernel Room | 20:00 Hours

The Bunker was silent, except for the hum of the cooling fans. The "Kernel Room" was a small annex off the main Ops Center, soundproofed and windowless. It contained a single table, two chairs, and a projector.

JD sat in one chair. Alex sat in the other.

"You look like a man who just spent seven hours watching paint dry," JD said, his face illuminated by the glow of a single lamp.

"Worse," Alex said, rubbing his temples. "I spent seven hours at the Country Club. Drinking liquid sugar and listening to

Bob Henderson explain the intricacies of doing absolutely nothing."

"And how did that make you feel?"

"Homicidal," Alex said. "And then sad. They look at me like I'm the problem. Like I'm the one who can't let go. But looking at them... they're just ghosts haunting their own lives."

JD nodded slowly. He opened a leather notebook. It wasn't a computer; it was paper. Analog security.

"Sun Tzu said, 'Know the enemy and know yourself,'" JD began. "We've spent the last week dissecting the enemy. The market. The noise. The institutions. We know the terrain."

He tapped the notebook with a pen.

"But today, we have to talk about the one variable you have been ignoring."

Alex leaned forward. "My money?"

"No," JD said sharply. "You."

"Me?"

"The Operating System," JD said. "You can have the best data, the fastest computers, and the most brilliant team in the world. But if your Kernel is corrupted, the whole system crashes."

He clicked a button on a remote. The projector flickered to life against the wall. It displayed a simple equation:

OUTPUT = (INPUT) x (KERNEL)

"In computing, the Kernel is the core component of an operating system," JD explained. "It bridges the software to the hardware. It manages the input/output requests."

"In life," JD continued, "your Kernel is your Value Algorithm. It is the set of assumptions and beliefs that filters every decision you make."

He looked at Alex. "Bob Henderson has a Kernel. His Kernel is Safety. Every piece of data that comes in, whether it's a stock tip, a vacation idea, or a career opportunity, gets filtered through 'Is this safe?' If the answer is no, he rejects it. His output is a life of safety."

"And what is my Kernel?" Alex asked.

"That's the problem," JD said. "Right now, your Kernel is Undefined. You are running on the default settings provided by the Pentagon. 'Obey orders.' 'Protect the unit.' 'Minimize risk to personnel.' But you are no longer in the Pentagon. You are in the private sector. And that Kernel is actively working against your wealth."

Alex thought about the Long Beach port. About the adrenaline he felt breaking the blockade.

"I think my Kernel is 'Action,'" Alex said.

"Action isn't a Kernel," JD countered. "Action is an output. Action comes from the desire for Control. Or perhaps the fear of Irrelevance."

He stood up and walked to the wall, where a list of words was written.

SECURITY LEGACY STATUS AUTONOMY IMPACT

"These are the five primary Kernels of the wealthy," JD said. "Most people are running on Security. The second tier is Status, buying the Ferrari to show they made it. The third is Legacy, building a library with their name on it."

He pointed to the last two. "But the Sovereign Wealth Command operates on the intersection of Autonomy and Impact."

He looked at Alex. "You don't want a yacht, Alex. You don't want a library. You want to command your own destiny. You want to build things that change the world. That is your Kernel: Sovereign Impact."

"So, what happens if I run a 'Safe' portfolio with a 'Sovereign Impact' Kernel?"

"System Failure," JD said instantly. "The friction burns you out. You make money, but you feel trapped. Or you lose money trying to force a safe investment to be exciting."

JD leaned in close. "This is the secret nobody talks about, Alex. Financial planning is generic. They assume everyone wants 'Wealth Preservation.' But you cannot preserve what you haven't yet built. And you cannot build without a defined purpose."

He tossed a pen onto the table.

"Write down your Kernel," JD commanded. "Not in business school words. In plain English. What is the one thing you must have to feel alive?"

Alex picked up the pen. He stared at the blank paper.

He thought about the port. The container. The deal with Aether Dynamics. He hadn't cared about the money. Not really. He had cared about the solution. He had cared about unlocking the chokepoint. He had cared about outsmarting the creditors.

He wrote: FLOW.

He looked at the word. It felt right.

"Flow?" JD asked. "As in cash flow?"

"No," Alex said. "As in the state of being completely immersed in an activity. When I was a commander in the field, time didn't exist. There was only the mission. The logistics. The flow of information. I want that feeling in my civilian life. I want to build systems that work like a well-oiled machine. I don't want to sit on a beach. I want to build the beach."

JD read the word. He smiled. A rare, genuine smile.

"Flow is a powerful Kernel," JD said. "It accepts risk. It demands growth. It rejects stagnation."

He picked up a red marker. "Okay. We have the Kernel: FLOW."

"Now we test it."

***

Location: The Rivera Residence | The Living Room | 21:30 Hours

Alex arrived home to find the lights on, and Martin Sterling's silver Audi parked in the driveway.

His stomach tightened. This wasn't a scheduled meeting. This was an ambush.

He walked inside. Elena, Martin, and a younger woman in a sharp grey suit were sitting in the living room. There was a bottle of wine on the coffee table, half empty. They were laughing.

"Alex!" Elena said, her voice bright. A little too bright. "Martin brought his colleague, Sarah. She's an Estate Planning specialist."

Martin stood up, beaming. "Alex! We were just catching up. Sarah was telling us about this amazing opportunity. Very exclusive. Very secure."

Alex looked at the younger woman, Sarah. She looked like a shark wearing lipstick.

"I was just explaining to Elena," Martin said, "that we need to be careful. With the volatility in the markets, did you see the tech drop today? Terrible business, we need to shelter your assets. We're looking at a Structured Annuity with a Guaranteed Lifetime Income Rider."

He paused for effect. "It pays out 5%, guaranteed. No matter what the market does."

Alex looked at Elena. She was nodding. "It sounds safe, Alex. And the tax benefits..."

The room felt like the inside of a submarine. The walls were closing in.

Alex sat down. He felt the weight of the "Flow" Kernel in his pocket, the paper he had written in The Bunker.

"Five percent," Alex said. "Guaranteed."

"Guaranteed," Martin confirmed. "It's backed by the insurer's general account. Very strong balance sheet. A-rated."

"And what are the terms?" Alex asked. "If I need the money for something else? If I find an investment opportunity?"

Martin frowned. "Well, there are surrender charges. Ten percent for the first seven years. It's a long-term commitment, Alex. You're locking in your peace of mind."

There it was. The trap.

The annuity promised safety. But the "Surrender Charges" were a cage. Once Alex locked his money into that 5% contract, he was done. He couldn't deploy capital to Long Beach. He couldn't invest in Aether Dynamics. He couldn't flow.

He would be a hostage to his own money.

"It's a great product for retirees," Alex said slowly. "But I'm not retiring."

Martin sighed. He looked at Elena. "We talked about this, Elena. He's having trouble letting go. It's common."

Elena looked at Alex, her eyes pleading. "Alex, please. Just listen. We need to think about the kids. The house. Stability."

Alex looked at his wife. He saw the fear. It wasn't greed; it was the fear of losing the Home Theater. The fear that his "Flow" would capsize their boat.

He took a deep breath. He didn't argue the math. You don't argue math with a spreadsheet. You argue values.

"Martin," Alex said, his voice dropping into the Command Register. "What is the highest return you have ever generated for a client in a single year?"

Martin blinked. "Well, in a bull market... maybe twelve percent. But that's variable. The annuity is guaranteed."

"And what is the most valuable thing you own, Martin?" Alex asked.

"My partnership in the firm," Martin said, puffing his chest slightly.

"If I offered you a guaranteed 5% return to buy your partnership today, but you had to give up your voting rights, your office, and your ability to make decisions... would you do it?"

Martin laughed nervously. "That's not a fair comparison."

"It's exactly the same," Alex said. He turned to Elena. "Elena, this product isn't an investment. It's a prison."

"Alex!" Elena snapped.

"Hear me out," Alex said. He pulled the paper from The Bunker out of his pocket. He unfolded it.

"We've been trying to build a financial plan based on Fear," Alex said. "Fear of the market. Fear of running out of money. That's Martin's plan. It's a plan to minimize the downside. But minimizing the downside also kills the upside."

He pointed to the word he had written: FLOW.

"I have realized something about myself," Alex said, looking Elena in the eye. "I am not a 'preserve' asset. I am a 'growth' asset. My value comes from movement. From action. From solving problems."

He looked at Martin. "If I lock my money into your annuity, I lose my liquidity. I lose my ability to command. If I lose that, I lose the thing that makes me successful. And if I lose that, the money I 'saved' becomes meaningless."

Martin shook his head. "You're gambling on yourself, Alex. That's risky."

"No," Alex said, his voice like steel. "I'm investing in myself. That's the difference between a consumer and a Commander."

He looked at the young woman, Sarah. "Sarah, tell me. Does that annuity allow me to withdraw 100% of my liquidity in 24 hours if I find a distressed asset with a 300% return?"

She hesitated. "No. Absolutely not."

"Then it's useless to me," Alex said. "Because I just found one of those."

The room went silent.

Elena stared at him. "What are you talking about?"

Alex smiled. It was the smile of a man who had just decoded the enemy's signal. "The Long Beach deal. The Aether Dynamics container. We closed it this afternoon. The equity stake is going to be worth more than five years of your annuity payments."

Martin's jaw dropped. "You... you did what? You invested in a shipping container?"

"I executed a strategic intervention," Alex corrected. "I unlocked a chokepoint. I created value."

He turned back to Elena. "That's what I do, Elena. I don't garden. I build gardens. I don't watch the waves. I learn to sail."

He stood up. The air in the room had shifted. The fear was gone, replaced by the electric buzz of possibility.

"We are not buying the annuity," Alex said. It wasn't a question.

Martin started gathering his papers, his face flushed a deep red. "You're making a mistake, Alex. The market eats people like you. You're not special. You're just a middle-aged man with a pension."

"Perhaps," Alex said, walking him to the door. "But I'm a middle-aged man who knows his Kernel."

He opened the door. The night air was cool.

"Goodnight, Martin. Drive safe."

When he came back to the living room, Elena was sitting on the sofa, looking at the glass of wine.

"You really made a deal?" she whispered.

"Yes," Alex said, sitting next to her. "And it's going to work."

"How do you know?"

"Because I stopped trying to be someone I'm not," Alex said. "I stopped trying to fit into Bob Henderson's golf shoes. I'm accepting who I am."

He took her hand.

"I'm not going to be safe, Elena," he said. "I'm going to be formidable. And that is the only safety I believe in."

She looked at him for a long time. Then, for the first time in months, she squeezed his hand back.

"Okay," she said. "Commander."

***

Lesson Learnt:

- Military Doctrine: The Kernel. Every OS has a core set of instructions that dictates how it processes data. You cannot run a "Sovereign Impact" strategy on a "Safety" Kernel. The internal conflict will cause you to self-sabotage. You must define your operational doctrine first.

- Financial Doctrine: The Identity Asset. Most financial plans treat the individual as a generic variable (a "risk profile"). In reality, the individual is the most valuable asset class they own. If your financial strategy requires you to suppress your core nature (e.g., forcing a builder to sit still), you are destroying your primary asset. Align your capital with your identity. Do not play to minimize loss; play to maximize your specific leverage.

Chapter 7: The Terrain of Opportunity

Location: The Rust Belt | Former Industrial District of Baltimore | 10:00 Hours

The air in Baltimore smelled of wet asphalt and history. Old history. The kind that rusted.

Alex Rivera stood in the middle of a parking lot, the size of a football field. He was staring at a building that looked like it had lost a fight with a depression-era steamroller. It was a brutalist slab of concrete, stained with soot, its windows shattered like a boxer's teeth.

"This," Sanjay Mehta said, throwing his arms wide as if presenting the Mona Lisa, "is the Cathedral of the Future."

Alex kicked a piece of loose asphalt. It skittered across the lot and hit a rusted shopping cart. "Sanjay, this isn't a cathedral. It's a tomb. It's a zombie mall. The Sears closed in 2010. The

JCPenney closed in 2015. There are probably things living in that HVAC system that haven't been classified by science."

"Don't be a philistine," Sanjay said, dancing around a puddle of oily water. He was wearing a white suit, which was a bold choice for an industrial wasteland. "You're looking at the surface layer. You're looking at the skin. I'm looking at the bones."

Sanjay tapped a tablet he was holding. A 3D blueprint overlaid the dilapidated building in augmented reality. Clean lines. Glass walls. A fortress.

"The structural integrity is A-plus," Sanjay said. "Reinforced concrete. Six-inch floor slabs. It was built during the Cold War as a fallout shelter that could transform as a department store. It's a bunker, Alex. A bunker with great parking."

Alex walked to the edge of the building. He placed his hand on the rough concrete. It was cold. Solid.

"Okay," Alex admitted. "It's defensible. Good sightlines. But we're not fighting the Soviets, Sanjay. We're building wealth. Where's the profit? Who shops here?"

"Nobody," Sanjay said, grinning. "That's the point."

He pulled up a map. A glowing blue line ran diagonally across the parking lot, cutting right through the abandoned Sears entrance.

"This," Sanjay said, pointing at the line, "is the main fiber-optic trunk line for the entire Eastern Seaboard. It runs underground. Right there."

Alex looked at the cracked asphalt. "So?"

"So," Sanjay said, "we are not buying a mall. We are buying a node. Amazon, Google, Azure, they are desperate for 'Edge Computing' centers. They need servers close to the population centers, but they can't build downtown because the NIMBYs scream about the noise and the traffic."

Sanjay spun around. "But here? In the Rust Belt? In a zombie mall? The mayor will give us the land for a dollar just to get it back on the tax rolls. We buy this shell, we gut the interior, and we turn it into a server farm."

Alex looked at the building again. The shift in perspective was jarring. He wasn't looking at a retail failure anymore. He was looking at infrastructure.

"It's a Terrain Play," Alex murmured. "Finding value in the geography, not the business."

"Exactly," Sanjay said. "The Terrain of Opportunity."

Just then, a sleek black limousine rolled slowly into the parking lot. It maneuvered around the potholes like a predator stalking prey, crunching gravel, until it came to a halt a few feet away.

The window rolled down. A man in his sixties, wearing a fedora and a trench coat, stared out. He looked like he had stepped out of a 1940s noir film.

Sanjay stiffened. "Oh, hell."

"Who is that?"

"Victor Kogan," Sanjay whispered. "The Walrus of Wall Street. He's a slum lord. He buys old industrial sites, waits for the city to restore, and then flips them to luxury developers."

The door opened, and Victor Kogan stepped out. He was a mountain of a man, broad and soft, smelling of expensive cologne and cigar smoke. He walked with a cane, tapping it on the asphalt.

"Mr. Mehta," Kogan rumbled. His voice was like gravel in a cement mixer. "I see you still like to play with garbage."

"Mr. Kogan," Sanjay said, his voice tight. "I prefer to think of it as recycling."

Kogan laughed. It was a wet, ugly sound. "This property is already spoken for, sonny. I have the option agreement with the city. I'm going to put up high-rises. Luxury apartments with river views. The yuppies will love them."

Alex stepped forward. "Apartment buildings require zoning changes, environmental impact studies, and infrastructure upgrades. The water lines in this district are a hundred years old."

Kogan turned his gaze to Alex. He looked him up and down, dismissing him instantly. "And you are? The chauffeur?"

Alex didn't blink. "I'm the competition."

Kogan sneered. "Competition requires capital, boy. I have liquidity. I have permits. I have the mayor on speed dial."

He tapped the building with his cane. "You can't play this game. You're looking for the quick flip. I'm building an empire."

Alex looked at the rusted mall, then at the fiber map on Sanjay's tablet, then at Kogan.

Kogan was right about one thing. He had the money. He had the permits. If they got into a bidding war, the Walrus would crush them.

But Alex noticed something. He looked at the roof of the building. It was flat. Massive. And it was surrounded by three-story industrial buildings, creating a natural wind tunnel.

"Sanjay," Alex said quietly, not taking his eyes off Kogan. "Does the fiber line connect to the building?"

"Not yet," Sanjay said. "You need a splice point. That's the tricky part. It costs a fortune to dig up the street."

Alex nodded. He turned to Kogan. "You're going to build luxury apartments here?"

"That's what I said."

"Good luck with the heat," Alex said casually. "Those servers, if they were there, would pump out enough heat to keep a block warm. But you're building condos. So, I assume you've checked the electrical load?"

Kogan frowned. "Electrical load is fine. We'll upgrade the grid."

"It's not the grid," Alex said, lying with the confidence of a prophet. "It's the geology. This whole block is built on a landfill. The ground is unstable."

Kogan paused. He was a predator, and predators were easily spooked by signs of weakness.

"Landfill?" Kogan asked.

"The methane leeching is intense," Alex continued, walking toward the edge of the lot. He pointed at a random patch of dead grass. "See that? The soil is toxic. If you dig a foundation for a high-rise, you're going to hit a pocket of gas. You'll spend ten years fighting the EPA."

Kogan walked over. He looked at the grass. He sniffed the air. (It was just exhaust, but fear smelled like whatever you wanted it to).

"I didn't see this in the survey," Kogan grumbled.

"It's in the deep scans," Alex said. "We only looked because we were planning a low-impact facility. A data center. We don't need deep foundations. We just need the slab."

Kogan stared at the dead grass. His eyes narrowed.

"A data center," Kogan mused. "Those things make noise. The residents will complain."

"Not if we sell it to Amazon," Alex said. "Amazon writes checks. They don't complain."

Kogan turned to his driver. "Check the EPA reports for this site. Look for soil contamination."

The driver nodded and pulled out a phone.

Kogan looked back at Alex. For the first time, there was a glint of respect in those porcine eyes. "You're a sharp operator, Mr...?"

"Rivera," Alex said. "And I know when to hold, and when to fold."

Kogan grunted. "The terrain wins, son. Always."

The limo backed up and drove away, the tires spinning slightly in the gravel.

Sanjay let out a breath he had been holding for three minutes. "There is no methane leak, Alex. If he digs deep, we're screwed."

"We'll have closed the deal by then," Alex said. "And you know what?"

"What?"

"I actually liked the sound of that. 'The terrain wins.'"

***

Location: The Bunker | The Digital Sandbox | 14:00 Hours

The Bunker was humming with a different kind of energy today. Maya had covered the maps of the world with a glowing, neon lattice. It looked like a subway map for a city that didn't exist.

Alex walked in, still dusting off his suit from the Baltimore site.

"You played him," Maya said, not looking up from her screens. "Kogan. You used the psychological advantage. Very Sun Tzu."

"It wasn't a trick," Alex said. "It was terrain analysis. He saw a vertical play (build up). We saw a horizontal play (build out). But the key was the pipe. The fiber."

Maya spun around in her chair. "You're starting to see the invisible layers. That's good."

JD stepped out of the shadows. He was wearing a construction worker's hard hat, which was so out of character Alex stopped in his tracks.

"Nice hat, General," Alex said.

"It's a visual aid," JD said, tapping the plastic crown. "We are talking about Terrain today, Alex. And the biggest mistake investors make is thinking terrain only exists in the physical realm."

He pointed to the glowing lattice on the screen.

"Physical terrain is easy," JD said. "It's land. It's gold. It's oil. You can touch it. You can hold it. The old generals, your Bob Henderson types, they love physical terrain. It feels real. It feels safe."

He took off the hard hat and placed it on a server rack.

"But the future war is being fought on the Digital Terrain."

Alex looked at the screen. "You mean stocks? Crypto?"

"I mean infrastructure," JD corrected. "The digital layer of the world is the new geography. The physical world is just the user interface. The real money flows through the wires."

Maya typed a command. The lattice shifted. A single red node appeared in the middle of the web.

"This," she said, "is a domain name. A .com address. A piece of digital real estate that doesn't exist physically but controls the traffic for a million dollars of business."

"And this," she said, shifting the view again, "is a block of IPv4 addresses."

"I know what IP addresses are," Alex said. "They're like phone numbers for computers."

"They are finite," Maya said. "And they are running out. Owning a block of IP addresses is like owning a toll booth on the information superhighway. Every piece of data that flows through that digital territory pays a toll to the owner."

Alex felt the concept clicking into place. It was the same as the shipping container. It was the same as the railroad barons of the 1800s.

"Control the flow," Alex said.

"Control the flow," JD agreed. "You bought the mall in Baltimore because it sits on top of the pipe. That's Physical Terrain intersecting with Digital Terrain. The Convergence."

JD walked to the whiteboard. He drew a circle.

"Most financial advisors tell you to diversify across Asset Classes. Stocks. Bonds. Real Estate. That is 1980s thinking."

He drew a line cutting through the circle.

"We tell you to diversify across Terrain Layers."

Layer 1: The Substrate. (Earth, Water, Power, Rare Earth Metals). This is the physical layer. Layer 2: The infrastructure. (Fiber, Satellites, Shipping Routes, IP Blocks). This is the transport layer. Layer 3: The Application. (Software, Platforms, Content, Brands). This is the visible layer.

"The retail investor buys Layer 3," JD explained. "They buy Apple stock. They buy Netflix. They buy the flashy logo on the screen. That's volatile. That's fashion."

" Institutions and governments fight over Layer 1," JD continued. "They fight over the copper mines and the oil fields."

"But where is the Sweet Spot?" Alex asked.

"The Sweet Spot," JD said, tapping the middle circle, Layer 2, "is the logistics. The infrastructure. The 'Pipe.'"

He looked Alex in the eye. "The mall in Baltimore is a Layer 1 asset. The fiber line underneath it is a Layer 2 asset. But the building itself? The physical structure? That's the interface."

He paused for effect.

"The internet is becoming physical," JD said. "As we move into the era of AI, the AI needs to live somewhere. It needs massive power. Massive cooling. Massive data pipes. The companies that own the AI software are valuable. But the people who own the ground the AI sits on? The real estate of the digital world?"

JD leaned in. "They are the Kings of the new economy."

Alex looked at the photo of the Baltimore mall on his phone. The rotting concrete, the broken windows.

He wasn't seeing a ruin anymore. He was seeing a castle. A castle built on top of a goldmine.

"The Walrus wanted to build apartments," Alex said, shaking his head. "He wanted to sell shelter to people who don't want to live there."

"He didn't see the pipes," Sanjay said, eating a donut. "He was looking at the skin. You looked at the blood."

"Kogan will be back," Alex said. "Once he realizes there's no methane, or once he figures out why we want it."

"He can have the apartments next door," JD said dismissively. "Let him deal with the zoning boards and the plumbing inspections. Let him fight the war for the surface. We want the subterranean."

"We are going to build the Digital Fortress," JD said. "And we are going to start with that mall."

Alex smiled. He felt the thrill of the hunt. He hadn't fired a shot, but he had just secured a strategic objective.

"I need to call Elena," Alex said. "Tell her I'm buying a shopping center."

"She'll love that," Maya said sarcastically. "Just tell her it's an investment in the 'Cloud.' Girls love the Cloud."

***

Location: The Rivera Residence | The Patio | 19:00 Hours

The sun was setting over the backyard, casting long, golden shadows across the lawn. Elena was sitting at the patio table, looking at a stack of documents that was thick enough to stop a bullet.

Alex opened a beer and sat down opposite her. He placed a folder on top of the stack.

"Please tell me," Elena said, rubbing her temples, "that this isn't another investment in a shipping container."

"No containers," Alex said. "Just... land."

"Land is good," Elena said, her shoulders relaxing slightly. "Where? A farm? A vineyard?"

"A mall," Alex said.

Elena froze. She picked up the folder. She opened it. She stared at the photos of the graffiti-covered walls, the broken skylights, and the weedy parking lot.

"Alex," she said, her voice dangerously calm. "Are you pranking me? Is there a camera somewhere?"

"It's a data center site," Alex said, leaning forward. "Look at the location map."

He flipped to a page that showed the proximity to the highway and the fiber lines.

"It's a zombie mall," Elena said. "It's where drug dealers go to die."

"It's where the internet lives," Alex countered. "Elena, listen to me. The world is changing. We aren't fighting for office space anymore. We are fighting for Infrastructure."

He pointed to the map. "This isn't a retail property. This is a logistics node. It's a piece of the new terrain."

Elena looked at him. She saw the intensity in his eyes. She hadn't seen that look in a decade. He didn't look like a retired man trying to find a hobby. He looked like a Commander briefing a subordinate.

"And what about Kogan?" she asked, naming the name on the option agreement. "The seller said a developer was interested."

"We handled Kogan," Alex said with a ghost of a smile. "He's going to build condos next door. Our property will be the server hub for his complex."

Elena looked back at the photos. She was a lawyer. She knew how to read a contract. She looked at the price. It was... surprisingly low.

" Why is it so cheap?" she asked.

"Because everyone else is looking at the surface," Alex said. "They see a dead mall. They see the Peace Dividend failure. I see a fortress."

He reached across the table and took her hand.

"This isn't a gamble, Elena. This is the beginning of the Sovereign Infrastructure. We are going to own the pipe. We are going to own the road."

Elena stared at the graffiti in the photo. Then she looked at Alex. She saw the man she married, the man who could navigate a minefield in the dark.

She closed the folder.

"If I see one graffiti artist on the premises," she said, "I'm sending you in there with a pressure washer."

Alex laughed. "Deal."

He took a sip of his beer. The evening air was cool. The sun was gone, and the stars were coming out.

He thought about the map of the world on Maya's screen. The glowing lattice of the internet.

He thought about the terrain of the future.

For years, he had fought on hills and deserts. Now, he was fighting on fiber and concrete. It was all terrain. It was all logistics.

And he was building his road to victory.

***

Lesson Learnt:

- Military Doctrine: The Center of Gravity. Every terrain has a focal point, the key position that, if held, allows you to control the surrounding area. In modern finance, the Center of Gravity is shifting from tangible assets (buildings) to the Logistics of Intangibles (fiber, data centers, digital addresses).

- Financial Doctrine: The Layers of Terrain.

  1. Substrate: Physical resources (Land, Power, Chips).

  2. Infrastructure: The transport of value (Fiber, IP addresses, Blockchain ledgers).

  3. Application: The visible products (Apps, Stocks).

The Insight: Most investors crowd into Layer 3 (Applications/Stocks) because it is visible and easy to understand. The Sovereign Wealth Commander looks for Layer 2 opportunities, owning the infrastructure that the digital world depends on. Buy the toll booth, not the car. Buy the mall that houses the servers, not the website running on the servers.

Chapter 8: The Logistics of Sovereignty

Location: First National Bank of Virginia | Branch Manager's Office | 11:00 Hours

The carpet in Mrs. Gable's office was a shade of beige that could only be described as "apathy gray." It was the color of a Monday.

Alex Rivera sat in a vinyl chair that squeaked every time he shifted his weight. Across the mahogany desk, which was scratched and polished in equal measure, sat Mrs. Gable. She was a woman of a certain age, wearing a cardigan that looked like armor and glasses that magnified her eyes to a predatory size.

On her desk was a stack of paperwork. It was tall enough to stop a small-caliber bullet.

"The problem, Mr. Rivera," Mrs. Gable said, tapping the stack with a manicured fingernail, "is collateralization."

Alex looked at the paperwork. It was the loan application for the Baltimore Mall project.

"I have the property," Alex said, keeping his voice level. "I have the contract. I have the equity."

"But you don't have the liquidity," Mrs. Gable countered, beaming a smile that showed no teeth. "You see, according to our algorithms, your assets are... illiquid."

"Illiquid?"

"A pension is not cash," she said, enunciating every syllable. "Real estate is not cash. Even your recent investment in Aether Dynamics is stock. That's not cash. We need cash-on-hand. We need a debt-to-income ratio that suggests you could pay us back if the world ended tomorrow."

"General Patton didn't bring cash to the battle," Alex said, losing the battle against his temper. "He brought tanks and fuel. That's what I have. Assets."

"Mr. Rivera," she sighed, the sigh of a tired saint dealing with a delinquent child. "This isn't war. It's banking. We have a fiduciary duty to our depositors. We cannot authorize a twenty-million-dollar construction loan for a retired military officer with", she checked her screen, "no traditional W-2 income."

"I have income," Alex said. "I have distributions. I have dividends."

"Sporadic," she said, waving a dismissive hand. "Unpredictable. You might as well tell me you're paid in lottery tickets."

She pushed the stack of paper toward him. "I can offer you a home equity line of credit on your house. Perhaps fifty thousand dollars. That's enough for a nice renovation on the patio."

Alex looked at the fifty-thousand-dollar offer. He needed five million by Friday to start the excavation for the server farm cooling systems. If he didn't break ground, the city would revoke the permits. Kogan was circling like a vulture, waiting for the paperwork to expire.

"Mrs. Gable," Alex said, standing up. "Do you know what a supply line is?"

She blinked. "I beg your pardon?"

"In the military, a supply line is the lifeline," Alex said. "If I cut the supply line, the division dies in three days. You are asking me to cut my own supply line. You are telling me that I have the tanks, I have the soldiers, and I have the objective, but I'm not allowed to use the fuel trucks."

"We are just following the regulations, Mr. Rivera," she said, stiffening.

"You're following a script designed for a slow economy," Alex said. "The world moves at the speed of light now. Your algorithms are running on a clock from 1950."

He picked up the paperwork.

"I'm not borrowing fifty thousand dollars," Alex said. "And I'm not asking for permission anymore."

"Mr. Rivera, if you leave now—"

"I'm not leaving," Alex said. "I'm withdrawing my business."

He walked to the door.

"We don't have any business with you!" she called out. "You don't have any accounts here!"

He stopped. He looked back at her. He didn't smile. He didn't frown. He just looked at her with the cold, flat stare of a man who has seen things that would make her cardigan melt.

"I know," Alex said. "But I was going to move my pension rollover here. About three million dollars."

The silence in the room was absolute. The air conditioning hummed aggressively.

Mrs. Gable's mouth opened slightly.

"I think," Alex said, "I'll take that liquidity elsewhere. Somewhere they understand the difference between a vault and a prison."

He walked out.

***

Location: The Bunker | The Velocity Room | 13:00 Hours

The Bunker was vibrating. Not from the HVAC, but from the sheer speed of the data flowing through the servers. Sanjay had a bank of monitors set up that looked like the engine room of the Starship Enterprise.

"They still use mainframes?" Sanjay was laughing, his fingers ran across three keyboards. "First National of Virginia? Their core banking software was written in COBOL. COBOL, Alex! That's like trying to fly an F-35 with a propeller engine."

Alex paced the room. He was still angry about the meeting. The feeling of impotence. It was worse than losing a battle; it was being told you weren't even allowed to match up.

"They froze me out," Alex said. "They have the money, but they won't let it move."

"Exactly," JD said. He was sitting on a stool, eating a sandwich wrapped in wax paper. He looked like a construction worker on a lunch break.

"Listen to me, Alex. The single most unspoken truth in the financial world is this: Wealth is not what you own. Wealth is how fast you can move what you own."

He pointed to a screen showing a jagged line graph. It wasn't a stock chart; it was a graph of velocity.

"This is the Logistics of Sovereignty," JD said, taking a bite of his sandwich. "Most people think being rich means having a big pile of gold. They are wrong. If you have a pile of gold, but it takes you three weeks and five court orders to get it out of the vault, you are not rich. You are a janitor guarding a museum."

Alex stopped pacing. "You're talking about Liquidity."

"I'm talking about Mobility," JD corrected. "Liquidity is what the bank offers you, a cup of water if you beg for it. Mobility is the ability to divert a river."

JD wiped his hands on a napkin. "In the military, you have the concept of Force Projection. The ability to move combat power to any point on the globe rapidly. Financial Sovereignty is just Force Projection applied to capital."

He gestured to Sanjay. "Show him the bridge."

Sanjay typed a command. The main screen dissolved into a 3D representation of the global banking system. It looked like a constellation, with nodes connecting New York, London, Singapore, and... the Cayman Islands.

"This is the Shadow Banking System," Sanjay said. "This is the internet of money. The banks Mrs. Gable works for? They are the local dirt road. This? This is the Hyperloop."

He highlighted a blue line connecting Aether Dynamics' account to a new entity Alex had never heard of: Rivera Holdings I (Cayman).

"We are setting up a credit line against your Aether stock," Sanjay explained. "But we aren't doing it through the bank. We're doing it through a Decentralized Finance (DeFi) liquidity pool. We are tokenizing your shares as collateral."

"In English," Alex said.

"We are using your stock as collateral to borrow stablecoins, digital dollars, instantly," Sanjay said. "No Mrs. Gable. No waiting period. No credit check."

"How fast?"

Sanjay tapped the 'Enter' key. "How fast is now?"

The screen flashed green.

TRANSACTION CONFIRMED. LIQUIDITY ACCESSED: $5,000,000. TRANSFERRED TO: DIGITAL VAULT 44-ALPHA.

"Five million dollars," Alex said, staring at the screen. "In three seconds."

"The bank would have taken thirty days," JD said. "And they would have denied you. Because they are in the business of hoarding. We are in the business of flowing."

"But the risk," Alex said, his military brain scanning for IEDs. "If the stock drops? The protocol forces a sale."

"Yes," JD admitted. "So, we manage the risk. We don't borrow 100%. We borrow 30%. It's called a conservative Loan-to-Value ratio. But the speed... the speed is the weapon."

Alex looked at the number on the screen. $5,000,000.

It felt different than the pension. The pension was a promise. This was a weapon. It was ammunition sitting in a clip, ready to be fired.

"I can pay the contractors," Alex said.

"You can pay them in ten minutes," Sanjay said. "You can pay them in Bitcoin, if you want."

"Don't do that," Alex warned. "The contractors like green paper."

"We can convert it," Sanjay said. "We can bridge it from the blockchain, to the Fed wire system, to their checking account. It's called 'Fiat On-Ramping.' It's the logistics of the modern war."

Alex walked to the screen. He put his hand on the glass.

"This is sovereignty," he whispered. "Not asking for a loan. Having the ability to execute."

"Don't get cocky," JD said, finishing his sandwich. "Mobility comes with its own dangers. When you move fast, you hit bumps. And sometimes, you crash."

He stood up and threw the wrapper in the trash.

"We have a situation," JD said, his voice dropping an octave. "The excavator companies? The one starting tomorrow?"

"Yeah? What about them?"

"They just got a cease-and-desist from the city," JD said. "It seems Kogan isn't done with us. He called in a favor at the Department of Public Works. He claims there's an endangered bird living on the roof of the Sears."

"A bird?" Alex asked, incredulous. "In a zombie mall?"

"A pigeon with a good lawyer," JD said. "The excavation is halted until a bio-survey can be done. That takes two weeks."

Alex felt the anger flare up again. It was a delaying tactic. It was a chokepoint.

"If we wait two weeks, the permits expire," Alex said. "Kogan knows that."

"He knows," JD said. "He's trying to suffocate your supply line."

"How do we clear the bird?" Alex asked.

"We don't kill the bird," JD said. "We buy the air."

"What?"

"The bird lives on the roof," JD said. "The roof is part of the property. But the air above the roof? That's federal jurisdiction, technically."

JD walked to a map. "I have a friend at the FAA. If we file a flight plan for a drone survey, a 'Critical Infrastructure Inspection', we can override the city zoning. Federal law supersedes local nuisance laws."

"Drone survey?" Alex asked.

"Big drone," Sanjay said, grinning. "Armed with LiDAR and thermal imaging. We fly it over the roof, we prove there's no bird nest, and we file the report with the judge."

"And if the judge doesn't listen?"

"Then we use the money," JD said. "We pay the contractors to stand by. But we pay them to stage a protest. A 'Workers for Economic Justice' protest."

"You want me to hire a protest?" Alex asked.

"No," JD said. "I want you to hire the media. You create a narrative. 'The City is killing jobs.' You use the press to squeeze the Mayor. Kogan has the politicians; we have the mob."

Alex looked at the logistics map. It was a web of connections. Money, Law, Media, Tech.

It wasn't just fighting anymore. It was... maneuvering.

"Okay," Alex said. "Launch the drone. Pay the contractors. And let's squeeze the Mayor."

***

Location: The Baltimore Mall Site | 16:30 Hours

The site was quiet. Too quiet. The chain-link fence rattled in the wind. There was no sound of engines. No movement of dirt.

Alex stood by the gate, watching the drone operators, two guys Sanjay had hired who looked like they were on leave from a video game tournament.

"Ready, Commander?" one of them asked, holding a controller that looked like it belonged in a fighter jet.

"Launch," Alex said.

The drone, a matte black quad-copter the size of a coffee table, buzzed to life. It lifted straight up, then shot forward like a missile, climbing rapidly.

Alex watched the screen on the operator's tablet. The camera fed back a grainy, green-tinted view of the roof. It was a wasteland of gravel and tar.

"Sector 4 clear," the operator said. "Sector 5 clear."

Suddenly, a black sedan pulled up to the fence. It was Kogan. He wasn't smiling today. He looked tired. And angry.

He stepped out of the car, leaning heavily on his cane.

"You think you're clever?" Kogan shouted over the hum of the drone. "You think you can just fly toys in the air?"

"I think I can do whatever I want," Alex said, turning to face him. "I own the air, Kogan. I own the ground. What do you own? A piece of paper from a zoning board?"

Kogan gripped the fence. "I have the law on my side, Rivera."

"The law is just ink on a page," Alex said. "Logistics is reality. The reality is, I have the money. I have the tech. I have the will."

He pointed up at the drone. "Right now, that drone is scanning for the bird. The one that doesn't exist. But even if it did exist... I would just pay the fine."

"You can't fight City Hall," Kogan spat.

"I'm not fighting them," Alex said. "I'm buying them."

Just then, Sanjay's phone buzzed. He answered, listened for a second, and nodded. He hung up.

"Mayor just called," Sanjay said, leaning against the fence, eating a bag of chips. "He said the bird complaint was 'reconsidered.' He's sending the inspectors out tomorrow."

Kogan's face turned a shade of purple usually reserved for bruised plums.

"How?" Kogan whispered.

"Because the Mayor realizes," Alex said, stepping closer to the fence, "that there are five million dollars of investment waiting to flood into his district if he gets out of the way. And he knows that if he blocks us, the next drone up there won't be taking pictures. It'll be carrying a news crew from CNN asking why the Mayor hates jobs."

Kogan stared at him. The realization dawned in his eyes. He wasn't fighting a developer. He was fighting a Commander.

"Enjoy your mall," Kogan said, turning back to his car. "You'll still fail. The power grid won't handle the load."

"We'll fix that too," Alex said. "We'll buy the grid if we have to."

The sedan peeled away, tires smoking.

Alex watched him go. The drone hummed overhead, a mechanical guardian circling the perimeter.

"So," Sanjay said, crunching a chip. "We're really doing this? The digital fortress?"

Alex looked at the desolate lot, the dead mall, the gray sky. He saw the future. He saw the servers humming. He saw the data flowing.

"We're not just building a data center," Alex said. "We're building a sovereign territory."

He pulled out his phone. He opened the app Sanjay had built. He pressed a single button: EXECUTE.

Somewhere in the Cayman Islands, algorithms churned. Somewhere in Baltimore, the excavator operator's phone buzzed with a notification: Deposit Received.

"Start the engines," Alex said.

The ground began to shake.

***

Lesson Learnt:

- Military Doctrine: Force Projection & Supply Lines. A General is only as powerful as his ability to project force to the battlefield. Static assets (tanks in the garage) are useless if you cannot move them to the front. Supply lines must be redundant, protected, and fast.

- Financial Doctrine: The Logistics of Sovereignty (Mobility > Liquidity). True wealth is not measured by the Net Worth statement (a static snapshot) but by the Velocity of Capital. If you cannot access your money in 24 hours, you are illiquid and vulnerable. Sovereign Wealth requires a "Shadow Banking" infrastructure, private credit lines, digital bridges, and off-balance-sheet vehicles, that allows you to bypass the bureaucratic friction of traditional banking. You must own the pipes, not just the water.

Chapter 9: Force Without Fighting

Location: The War Room | Downtown Washington D.C. | 09:00 Hours

The air inside the private conference room at the offices of Apex Energy Solutions was scrubbed, filtered, and chilled to exactly sixty-eight degrees. It smelled of ozone and expensive suits.

Alex Rivera sat on a leather chair that cost more than his first car. Opposite him sat Arthur Vane, the CEO of Apex. Vane was a man who looked like he had been carved out of granite and polished with articulation. He wore a tie that cost a month's rent, and he wasn't looking at Alex. He was looking at his phone, scrolling through emails with a thumb that moved with impatient precision.

"Mr. Rivera," Vane said without looking up. "I appreciate you coming. But I think you're confused."

"I'm not confused," Alex said. "I'm the bidder on the Grid Substation on the East Side."

Vane laughed. It was a short, sharp sound, like a glass breaking. "Bidder? You put in an offer. That's cute. But let's be clear about the physics here. You have twenty million dollars. I have four billion. In a resource war, the side with the most ammo wins. That's not a strategy. That's a fact."

Vane finally looked up. His eyes were cold. "The grid is a natural monopoly. The city knows this. They want the deep pockets. They want Apex. We can upgrade the infrastructure, absorb the losses for five years, and then price-gouge the consumers into the next century. It's the American way."

Alex didn't flinch. "You're going to strip the copper. You're going to defer maintenance. And when the next heatwave hits, the East Side is going to blackout."

"Capitalism is creative destruction, Captain," Vane said, emphasizing the rank with a sneer. "Sometimes things break. But the shareholders? They do very well."

He stood up. The meeting was over.

"Go back to your data center, Rivera. Buy your servers. But the power that runs them? That belongs to us now. We'll charge you whatever we want, and you'll pay it, because you'll have nowhere else to go."

Vane walked out of the room, leaving Alex alone with his twenty-million-dollar "loser" bid.

Alex sat there for a moment. He looked at the city skyline through the glass wall. He realized Vane was right. In a direct conflict, fistfight for fistfight, Alex would lose. He was a speedboat trying to ram a battleship. The battleship would just sink him without even noticing the scrape.

He needed to stop trying to ram the battleship.

He needed to become the ocean.

***

Location: The Bunker | The Strategy Pit | 13:00 Hours

Alex slammed the door of The Bunker open. He was angry. Not the cold, calculated anger of a commander, but the hot, frustrated rage of a man who had been told to sit at the kids' table.

Sanjay was hanging upside down from a pull-up bar, wearing a VR headset. "Did you win? Did you crush the capitalist pig-dog?"

"I got crushed," Alex said, pacing the floor. "Vane has four billion dollars. He's going to buy the grid, starve us out, and sell us electricity at a premium. The Baltimore project is dead before the first server boots up."

He kicked a crate. "We need to fight back. I can call in some favors. I know some guys in the Pentagon. Maybe we can launch an antitrust investigation?"

"Slow down, General," JD said. He was sitting in the corner, cutting a piece of wood with a pocketknife. "You want to fight him on his battlefield. He has the money. He has the lawyers. He has the politicians in his pocket."

"So, we surrender?" Alex snapped.

"Sun Tzu said, 'The supreme art of war is to subdue the enemy without fighting,'" JD said, not looking up from the wood. "Fighting is what you do when you have failed. Fighting is a failure of imagination."

He blew the wood shavings off the carving. It looked like a small bird.

"Vane thinks he is buying an asset," JD said. "He is buying a physical thing, cables, transformers, substations. He is playing 4D Chess in a 6D world."

JD tossed the wooden bird to Alex. "What does a power grid actually do?"

"It distributes electricity," Alex caught the bird.

"It enforces Compliance," JD corrected. "It ensures that the energy produced matches the frequency and voltage required by the devices. The grid is not just power; it is Law. It is a set of rules."

Maya spun her chair around. "Vane bought the wires. But who owns the protocols?"

Alex paused. "What?"

Sanjay flipped off his headset and dropped to the floor, landing lightly. "Think of it like the internet, Commander. Vane bought the fiber optic cable. But he doesn't own

TCP/IP. He doesn't own the language the computers use to talk."

"So?" Alex asked.

"So," Maya said, typing rapidly. "I've been looking at the Federal Energy Regulatory Commission (FERC) guidelines. There is a provision called 'Critical Infrastructure Reliability.' It states that any grid connected to a 'National Defense Asset' must adhere to Red-Level Security Standards."

Alex looked at her. "We aren't a National Defense Asset."

"Not yet," Sanjay grinned. "But what if we were?"

JD stood up. "Alex, you have a Top Secret clearance. You have the experience. And you have a building in Baltimore that is perfectly positioned to become a node for... let's say... a Federal Disaster Recovery Center."

"A disaster center?"

"If you offer to host a government backup node," JD said, his voice dropping to that conspiratorial whisper, "you are no longer a commercial client. You are a Partner in National Defense."

"And as a partner," Maya chimed in, "you qualify for a 'Direct Connect' bypass. You don't plug into Vane's grid. You plug directly into the Federal transmission backbone. The 'Strategic Power Reserve.'"

Alex's eyes widened. "The Feds have their own reserve?"

"They have a secret grid," JD said. "Designed to keep the government running if the civilian world collapses. It's a ghost network."

He walked to the map of Baltimore.

"If we can get your building classified as a Critical Node, Vane can't touch you. He can't regulate your power. He can't cut you off. In fact, by law, his grid has to support your load first in an emergency."

Alex looked at the map. The lines were redrawing themselves in his mind. The "Force Without Fighting."

He wasn't attacking Vane's money. He was attacking his jurisdiction. He was moving the game from the Commercial Marketplace (where Vane was a God) to the National Security Arena (where Vane was a civilian with no clearance).

"It's brilliant," Alex said. "But how do I sell it? I can't just walk into the Department of Energy and ask for a classified hook-up."

"No," JD said. "You don't ask. You offer."

"Offer what?"

"A solution to a problem they have," Sanjay said. "I found an RFP, Request for Proposal, from the DoE yesterday. They are terrified of an EMP attack on the East Coast. They want a 'Distributed Recovery Node' prototype. Somewhere that can survive a solar flare."

Sanjay pointed at Alex. "You have a building with a nuclear-grade generator. You have a fiber line. And you have a Commander who knows how to operate in a black-ops environment."

Alex stared at them. They weren't just building a business. They were weaponizing his past. They were taking his scars and selling them as armor.

"So, I let the government use my basement," Alex said. "And in exchange, they give me immunity from Vane."

"And," JD added, holding up a finger, "they pay you. Grant money. 'Strategic Infrastructure Grants.' Vane pays billions for the grid. You get paid billions to exist."

"We win without buying," Alex whispered. "We win by becoming necessary."

***

Location: The Department of Energy | The Eisenhower Executive Office Building | 15:00 Hours

The security was tighter than a drum-head. Alex had walked through magnetometers, surrendered his phone, and been escorted by a silent guard down a corridor lined with portraits of serious men from the 1970s.

He was here to meet a woman named Director Kline. The head of Infrastructure Resilience.

Alex walked into her office. It was stark. A metal desk. A map of the U.S. power grid taking up an entire wall, pinned with red flags.

Director Kline stood by the map, drinking black coffee from a ceramic mug. She looked like a woman who hadn't slept since the Obama administration.

"Captain Rivera," she said, turning. She didn't offer a hand. "I know your record. The Afghanistan extraction. The supply chain audits. You were good at moving things that didn't want to be moved."

"Thank you, Madam Director."

"But now you're a civilian," she said, walking behind her desk. "You want to play with the big boys in energy. My staff tells me you applied for the 'Critical Node' grant."

"I didn't apply for a grant," Alex said, standing at ease, hands clasped behind his back. "I'm applying for a mission."

Kline looked up. "A mission?"

"The grid is vulnerable, Madam Director," Alex said. He pointed to the map. "Apex Energy is holding the East Coast together with duct tape and prayers. They are optimizing for shareholder value. That means, they are stripping out redundancy to save money."

He took a step closer. "I have a facility in Baltimore. It is hardened. It has redundant power. It has a direct fiber line. I am turning it into a private data sanctuary."

"And?" Kline asked, unimpressed.

"And I am willing to designate it as a National Recovery Asset," Alex said. "In the event of a grid collapse, solar flare, EMP, cyberattack, my facility will remain online. I will offer the Federal Government full access to my server capacity and my backup power."

Kline narrowed her eyes. "Why? What's the catch?"

"No catch," Alex said. "I just need protection."

"From whom?"

"From Apex," Alex said bluntly. "They are trying to squeeze me out of the energy market. If I am a designated Federal Asset, they can't touch me. They can't cut my lines. They can't deny me interconnection. Federal pre-emption supersedes state utility commissions."

Kline stared at him. She took a sip of coffee. She was calculating. She knew Apex was a problem. She knew the grid was fragile. She needed leverage against the energy giants, but Congress wouldn't give her the budget to build new stations.

She needed a private volunteer. A mercenary with a patriotic streak.

"You're offering to build us a bunker on your own dime," Kline said, "just to spite Arthur Vane?"

"I'm offering to build a fortress," Alex corrected, "so that I can run my business without a knife to my throat. But a rising tide lifts all boats. If the lights go out in Washington, your server stays lit."

He let that hang in the air.

"If I grant this," Kline said slowly, "I am essentially giving you a license to print money. You become a utility unto yourself. You are outside their regulation."

"I am inside your regulation," Alex countered. "I will be subject to your inspections. Your security protocols. Your audits. You will own the keys to the front door, Ma'am. But I own the house."

Kline looked at the map, at the red flags marking the vulnerable Baltimore corridor.

If Alex did this, it solved her political problem. She got a hardened data center for free. If she refused, Alex went bankrupt, Vane consolidated the grid, and the government was still vulnerable.

It was a no-brainer. But it required bending the rules. It required a Commander who understood that the law was flexible when the Nation was at risk.

Kline put her coffee cup down. She picked up a pen.

"If you pass the security certification," she said, "I will approve the designation. But be warned, Captain. Once you are a node, you are a target. In a war, the infrastructure gets bombed first."

"Madam Director," Alex said, smiling with the dry wit of a man who had seen the elephant. "I have spent thirty years being a target. Being a target just means I'm doing something right."

She signed the paper. "Get your building hardened, Rivera. I'm sending my inspection team in the morning."

"Thank you, Ma'am."

Alex walked out of the Eisenhower Building. The sun was hitting the White House across the street. It looked like a postcard.

He checked his phone. One new message from Vane. "Enjoy the power while it lasts, Rivera. The cut-off order goes in tonight."

Alex tapped the screen, deleting the message.

Vane was playing Monopoly. He was buying hotels on Boardwalk.

Alex was playing Risk. He had just allied with the Gods.

He pulled out his phone and dialed JD.

"Tell the construction crew to double shift," Alex said. "And tell Sanjay to get ready. We need to install a Faraday cage around the server room. Federal specs."

"Done and done," JD said. "How did it go?"

"We didn't fire a shot," Alex said, walking down the steps of the Department of Energy, feeling lighter than air. "We just became essential."

"And Vane?"

Alex looked at the sky. He imagined Vane receiving the notification that the Baltimore site was now under Federal Protection.

"Vane," Alex said, "is about to learn that he isn't the shark in the water. He's just the chum."

He hung up.

It was the purest form of victory. Not by destroying the enemy, but by making the enemy irrelevant.

Alex Rivera wasn't a businessman. He wasn't a General.

He was a force of nature. And like the weather, you couldn't fight him. You could only prepare for him.

***

Lesson Learnt:

- Military Doctrine: Force Without Fighting (Asymmetric Advantage). The highest form of strategy is to subdue the enemy without engaging in direct battle. Direct conflict burns resources. Asymmetric advantage, using superior positioning, legal maneuvering, and regulatory moats, allows you to win by default.

- Financial Doctrine: Regulatory Arbitrage & Strategic Criticality. You cannot beat a giant competitor on their turf (pricing/production volume). You must move the battlefield. By aligning yourself with National Security interests, you obtain protection that money cannot buy. You trade "commercial flexibility" for "sovereign immunity." Let your competitors fight for market share; you fight for essentiality. If the market cannot function without you, you win without fighting.

Chapter 10: The Empty Fort Strategy

Location: The Grand Ballroom | The Jefferson Hotel | 20:00 Hours

The room smelled of old money, expensive perfume, and the metallic tang of fear disguised as confidence.

It was the "Capitalist's Gala," an annual gathering for the East Coast's financial elites. Men in tuxedos, that cost more than a mid-sized sedan, circulating with women in gowns that defied physics. The champagne flowed like water in a desert.

Alex Rivera stood near a potted palm, nursing a glass of flat ginger ale. He was wearing a rented tuxedo that was slightly too tight in the shoulders and too long in the sleeves. He had a piece of spinach stuck in his teeth, a calculated placement.

He looked exactly like a man who was out of his depth. He looked like a fish that had accidentally learned to walk and was now regretting it.

"General!" a voice boomed.

It was Arthur Vane. He approached with a predatory grin, a beautiful blonde on his arm who looked at Alex with the bored curiosity of a cat watching a moth.

"Mr. Rivera," Vane said, slapping Alex on the back hard enough to spill the ginger ale. "I heard a rumor."

"Good news or bad?" Alex asked, wiping his chin with a napkin, feigning clumsiness.

"That you're trying to buy that Baltimore mall," Vane laughed, a sound that drew the attention of a small circle of sycophants. "The zombie mall. That's adorable. It's very... nostalgic. Do you have a hobby? Restoration?"

"Everyone needs a hobby," Alex said, forcing a nervous smile. "I just thought... maybe a warehouse? Storage unit?"

"Storage?" Vane smirked. "Rivera, that land is toxic. The structural survey says the foundation is shifting. You're going to sink your pension into a pit of quicksand."

Around them, the circle of financiers chuckled. They were sharks tasting blood in the water. They loved a failure. It made them feel taller.

"I..." Alex looked down at his shoes. "I didn't know that. The survey said it was stable."

"The survey was paid for by the seller," Vane said dismissively. "I should know. I tried to buy it three years ago.

The environmental cleanup alone is ten million. You're going to be bankrupt by Christmas."

The blonde on Vane's arm giggled. "But maybe he can use it as a haunted house? For Halloween?"

The group roared with laughter. Alex stood there, taking it. He played the part of the humiliated fool perfectly. He bowed his head. He nodded. He let them mock him.

But inside, behind the mask of the clumsy retiree, his mind was a calm, calculating machine.

He knew the foundation was fine. He had seen the core samples. He knew the environmental cleanup was a myth, he had the EPA waiver signed by the Mayor in his pocket.

He was feeding them disinformation. He was letting them look at his fortress and see nothing but ruins.

"Enjoy your evening, Arthur," Alex said quietly, backing away. "I think I need to use the restroom. Too much excitement."

As he walked away, Vane's voice drifted over the crowd. "Desperate fool. Throwing good money after bad. Short his stock if you can find it, boys. He'll be margin-called by spring."

Alex entered the restroom. He checked the stalls. Empty. He locked the door.

He pulled a small, encrypted earbud from his pocket and popped it in.

"You're clear," Maya's voice whispered in his ear. "No one followed. The bug in Vane's lapel is transmitting clearly."

Alex looked at himself in the mirror. He fixed his tie. The clumsy desperation vanished from his face, replaced by the cold, hard stare of the Commander.

"Tell me," Alex whispered.

"He's meeting the short-sellers at the bar in ten minutes," Maya said. "He's coordinating a coordinated attack. He wants to crash Aether Dynamics and the Baltimore project simultaneously. He's going to spread rumors that the power grid is failing."

Alex washed his hands. The water was cold.

"Let him," Alex said. "The Empty Fort requires an invader."

***

Location: The Baltimore Mall Site | The East Wing | 10:30 Hours

The next morning, the sun beat down on the abandoned parking lot. The chain-link fence rattled in the wind. To the casual observer, the building was dead. Windows were broken. The loading docks were rusted shut.

But inside the East Wing, in what used to be the "Housewares" section, a different reality existed.

It was a vast space, illuminated by harsh white LED work lights. Where once refrigerators and washing machines had been displayed, now stood rows of black server racks. They were silent, cooling fans humming a low, monotonous note.

It was the Empty Fort.

To the outside world, this was a failure. To Vane, this was a money pit. But in here, in the shadows of the hollowed-out mall, the most valuable computing power in the mid-Atlantic was booting up.

Alex stood on the mezzanine level, overlooking the racks. Sanjay was below, frantically connecting fiber optic cables to the main distribution frame.

"The grid connection is live," Sanjay shouted up. "We're pulling from the Apex line. Vane has no idea we're siphoning his juice."

"He thinks the mall is empty," Alex said. "He thinks we're bankrupt. That is why he hasn't sent the lawyers to disconnect us."

"He sent them anyway," Sanjay said. "Check the gate."

Alex looked out through the grime-streaked window. A black sedan was pulling up. Three men in suits got out. One was holding a clipboard. They had the slick, aggressive look of corporate liquidators.

"Open the gates," Alex said.

"Are you nuts?" Sanjay asked. "They're here to evict us."

"Open the gates," Alex commanded, his voice echoing in the warehouse. "And then, meet me at the Loading Dock 4. Do not engage. Just watch."

Sanjay hesitated, then nodded. He tapped a button on his tablet. The automated gate at the far end of the lot rolled open.

The three liquidators marched in. They walked through the debris, kicking aside old shopping carts. They looked angry, expecting resistance. They expected armed guards or legal teams.

Instead, they found Alex standing at Dock 4, leaning against the concrete wall, holding a broom.

"Mr. Rivera?" the lead liquidator said, suspicious. "We have a court order to seize the assets for non-payment of the environmental lien."

Alex looked at them. He looked tired. He looked defeated. He swept the floor with the broom, pushing a pile of dust into the wind.

"Go ahead," Alex said, his voice weary. "Take what you want. The place is empty. There's nothing here."

The liquidator frowned. He walked past Alex into the warehouse. He shone his flashlight around. The vast space was empty, except for the far corner which was shrouded in hanging plastic tarps.

"What's under the plastic?" the liquidator asked.

"Old insulation," Alex said. "Asbestos. Dangerous stuff. Don't go under there unless you want to die."

The liquidator sneered. He walked over to the plastic. He shone his light. He saw the yellow hazard signs Alex had hastily taped to the plastic: DANGER: BIOHAZARD.

"Disgusting," the man said, pulling his collar up. He didn't go under. He didn't look behind the second layer of plastic where the servers hummed in a temperature-controlled vacuum.

He walked back to Alex. "This place is worthless. There's nothing to seize."

"Told you," Alex said, leaning on the broom. "Just a lot of dust."

"You're free to go," the liquidator said, losing interest. "We'll report to the bank that there are no recoverable assets."

"Thanks," Alex said. "Have a good day."

The men left. They got back in their car and drove away. They reported exactly what Vane wanted to hear: The project was a bust. It was empty. It was over.

They never saw the 200 megawatts of power flowing into the building. They never saw the fiber optics pulsing with encrypted data for the Department of Defense. They saw what Alex wanted them to see.

They saw an Empty Fort.

***

Location: The Bunker | The Strategy Room | 16:00 Hours

Alex sat in the central chair, his feet up on the console. JD was pouring tea from a cast-iron kettle. The tension in the room was gone, replaced by the electric buzz of a successful operation.

"Sun Tzu would be proud," JD said, setting the cup down. "The Empty Fort Strategy is the ultimate psychological weapon."

He walked to the screen. On it, a chart of Apex Energy's stock was visible. It was flat.

"Vane spent the morning bragging to the short-sellers," JD said. "He told them you were broke. He told them the mall was a toxic waste dump. He convinced them to bet against you."

"Good," Alex said. "Let them bet."

"They are selling your stock short," JD explained. "They are borrowing shares to sell them, hoping to buy them back later for pennies. They are betting on your failure."

"And what happens when the servers go live on Friday?" Alex asked.

"When the government announces that the Baltimore site is the primary backup node for the entire Eastern Seaboard," JD said, smiling, "the value of that real estate doesn't just go up. It explodes."

He pointed to the screen. "Vane and his friends have sold shares of a company that is about to become the most essential piece of infrastructure in the country."

"The Short Squeeze," Alex said.

"The mother of all squeezes," Sanjay chimed in, spinning in a chair. "They sold short at ten dollars. When the news hits, the stock opens at fifty. They have to buy it back at fifty. They lose everything."

Alex watched the flat line. He thought of the gala. The humiliation. The laughter.

"They thought they were sharks," Alex said quietly. "They thought they were smelling blood."

"They were," JD said. "They just didn't realize the blood was bait."

He poured another cup of tea.

"The Empty Fort works because of the arrogance of the enemy," JD said. "They cannot conceive that a man with limited resources would voluntarily open his gates. They assume fear. They assume you are hiding because you are weak."

He looked at Alex. "But you are not hiding. You are camouflaged."

Alex took a sip of the tea. It was smoky, earthy.

"I realized something at the gala," Alex said. "I was so angry when Vane laughed. I wanted to punch him. I wanted to show him the blueprints."

"And that would have been the end of us," JD said. "If you show your strength, the enemy adapts. They bring bigger guns. By showing your weakness, you invite them to walk into the trap."

"In the military," Alex said, "we call it deception. In finance, they call it 'misdirection.' But in life... in life, it's just privacy."

He looked at his team. Maya, Sanjay, JD.

"The world is a loud place," Alex said. "Everyone is screaming about their wins. They post their yachts on Instagram. They announce their deals on CNBC."

"But the Sovereign Commander," Alex continued, "doesn't need applause. He doesn't need the world to know he won. He just needs to win."

JD nodded. "True sovereignty is the ability to stand in the center of a hurricane and appear to be standing still."

On the screen, a notification popped up.

FEDERAL PRESS RELEASE SCHEDULED: FRIDAY 09:00 EST. TOPIC: CRITICAL INFRASTRUCTURE GRANT - BALTIMORE.

Alex smiled. He leaned back in his chair.

Vane was out there, shorting the stock, counting his millions, celebrating the death of a rival.

He was attacking a ghost. He was storming a castle that had been abandoned by the garrison, but booby-trapped by the engineers.

The Empty Fort was full.

And on Friday, the doors would close. And Vane would be on the wrong side of them.

***

Lesson Learnt:

- Military Doctrine: The Empty Fort Strategy. When outnumbered, do not hide behind walls. Open the gates. Appear weak and vulnerable. The enemy, driven by arrogance and the fear of an ambush, will hesitate. They will assume the strength you are hiding is overwhelming, and they will retreat without fighting.

- Financial Doctrine: Sovereign Opacity. In a world of algorithmic surveillance and data mining, transparency is a weakness. Privacy is the ultimate armor. If the market thinks you are a loser, they will let you acquire your assets in peace. If the market thinks your fort is empty, you can build an army inside it without taxation or regulation. Never let the enemy count your troops until it's too late for them to run.

Part III: The Boot Sequence

(Initializing the System)

Chapter 11: Boot Up Sequence

Location: The Rivera Residence | The Living Room | 05:30 Hours

The house was silent, the kind of deep, pre-dawn hush that usually preceded a major tactical operation. But Alex wasn't preparing to enter a hostile country. He was preparing to leave a safe one.

On the glass coffee table, a stack of documents lay illuminated by the harsh light of a single lamp. They weren't deployment orders. They were authorization forms. Liquidation forms. Transfer requests.

"Alex," Elena said, her voice trembling. "This is the college fund. This is the money for Sarah's first degree. Maybe her Master's."

Alex looked at his wife. She was wrapped in a bathrobe, holding a mug of tea with both hands like it was a life preserver.

"If we don't do this," Alex said, his voice steady, "Sarah won't need a Master's. She'll need a job."

"It's the last of the 'Safe' money," Elena whispered. "Once you hit 'Execute' on that tablet, we have no liquidity. No cushion. Just the bet."

"A bet requires luck, Elena," Alex said, picking up the tablet. The screen glowed with a single red button: INITIATE LIQUIDATION. "This is an initialization. We are rebooting our operating system."

He thought about the conversation with JD the night before.

"Most people run in 'Safe Mode'," JD had told him. "Safe Mode is what your computer does when it's broken. It runs slow. It disables the cool features. It tries to protect you, but it can't actually do any work."

Alex looked at Elena. "We've been running in Safe Mode for twenty years. We're putting money in a 401(k) that we can't touch without a penalty. We're buying a house that ties us to a location. We're saving for a future. That system is actively dismantling."

"The system?" Elena asked, wiping her eyes.

"The financial system," Alex said. "It's designed to keep you in the loading bar. You know the loading bar? The little bar that fills up while a video game loads?"

Elena nodded.

"Society is stuck at 99% loaded," Alex said. "We work our whole lives to fill the bar, waiting for the game to start. But the game never starts. The bar just resets when we die."

He tapped the screen. "This is the reboot. We are clearing the RAM. We are taking the energy that's tied up in 'Safe' assets, assets that yield 2%, 3%, 5%. and we're injecting them into the kernel. The Aether stock. The Baltimore infrastructure. The sovereign entity."

"Alex," Elena said, her voice cracking. "If this crashes... we lose the house."

"We won't lose the house," Alex said, locking eyes with her. "Because the house isn't our home anymore. It's a tool. And I am a tool user, not a tool."

"I'm scared, Alex."

"Good," Alex said gently. "Fear is just data. It's the nervous system telling you that you are alive. Panic is the problem. Panic is a glitch."

He placed his thumb on the biometric scanner.

"Are we booting up?" he asked.

Elena looked at the stack of paper. She looked at the man she had married, the man who had walked away from the Army, only to find another, more dangerous war to fight.

She reached out and placed her hand over his.

"Boot up," she said.

Alex pressed the button.

The screen flashed: PROCESSING. ASSETS LIQUIDATED: $485,000. TRANSFER DESTINATION: RIVERA HOLDINGS (CAYMAN). TRANSFER STATUS: COMPLETE.

The house felt different instantly. It felt lighter. And emptier. The safety net was gone. They were standing on the high wire without a net.

***

Location: The Bunker | The Clean Room | 11:00 Hours

The atmosphere in The Bunker was surgical. Sanjay had covered the walls with whiteboards filled with flowcharts and "IF/THEN" logic trees. He was wearing a pair of blue-light blocking glasses and vibrating with caffeine.

"Okay, listen up!" Sanjay shouted, clapping his hands. "We are done with the hardware. We are done with the real estate. Today, we install the Software. The Wealth Command OS Version 1.0."

He pointed to Alex, who was sitting in the "Subject Chair" in the middle of the room.

"Alex, your brain is currently running 'Civilian Service Pack 5'," Sanjay said. "This is bloated. It's full of bloatware, social anxiety, fear of authority, linear thinking, risk aversion. It's slow. It crashes under stress."

He picked up a giant rubber stamp.

"We are formatting you."

Alex laughed nervously. "Is this going to hurt?"

"Only your ego," Maya said from her console. She was typing furiously. "I'm scrubbing your digital footprint. Sanjay is scrubbing your financial footprint."

"I have deleted your Netflix subscription," Sanjay said, tapping the whiteboard. "Gone. Bloatware. You don't watch it; you just stare at it to numb your brain."

"I deleted the Amazon Prime app from your phone," Maya added. "No more dopamine hits from buying gadgets you don't need. You are a Sovereign Commander now. You don't buy toys; you acquire assets."

"I bought you a new phone," JD said, walking out of the shadows. He handed Alex a sleek, black device. It looked military grade.

"It has no social media," JD said. "No stock apps. No news feeds. It is a dumb terminal for the genius that is Maya."

Alex took the phone. It felt heavy. Dense.

"It's just a phone," Alex said.

"It's the interface," JD corrected. "The computer doesn't matter. The keyboard doesn't matter. The OS matters."

He walked to the whiteboard and wrote a single word in the center.

LOOP.

"There is a concept in computing called the 'Event Loop,'" JD said. "The system listens for an input, processes it, and outputs a result."

He turned to Alex. "Most people have a Reactive Loop."

- INPUT: "Stock market drops."
- PROCESS: "Panic."
- OUTPUT: "Sell everything."

JD drew a second circle below it.

"We are installing a Sovereign Loop."

- INPUT: "Stock market drops."
- PROCESS: "Identify inefficiency."
- OUTPUT: "Buy the dip."

"The difference," JD said, his voice echoing slightly in the concrete room, "isn't intelligence. It's the Kernel. It's the default setting."

Alex looked at the circles. It made sense. The financial world wanted him to be a thermometer, reacting to the temperature. A Sovereign Commander was a thermostat, he set the temperature.

"So, how do I install the loop?" Alex asked.

"We don't install it," Sanjay said. "We activate it."

He pointed to the main screen. It displayed a timer counting down from ten minutes.

"Ten minutes until the Baltimore servers go live," Sanjay said. "And ten minutes until the Government press conference announcing the 'Critical Node' designation."

"This is the Boot Sequence," Maya said. "The moment the system comes online, it will demand resources. It will draw power. It will draw cash."

"Four-eighty-five thousand dollars," Alex said. "That's what we have in the tank."

"That's your RAM," Sanjay said. "You have enough RAM to run the launch. But once the OS is running... you have to keep feeding it. You need a perpetual energy source."

"The cash flow," Alex said. "We need the servers to start earning."

"Exactly," JD said. "And the only way they earn is if the grid holds. If Vane cuts the power before the servers sync with the Federal backbone, the boot fails. The system crashes."

"And we're broke," Alex finished.

"We're not broke," JD corrected. "We're bankrupt. Big difference. Broke means you have no money. Bankrupt means you have no money and no hope. We have plenty of hope."

The timer hit 05:00.

"Positions," Alex said. His voice changed. The hesitation was gone. The "Civilian Service Pack" was purged.

Sanjay sat at his console. Maya at hers. JD stood behind Alex.

"Weaponize the bandwidth," Alex commanded. "Prepare to broadcast."

***

Location: The Baltimore Mall | Server Farm | 11:55 Hours

The silence in the old Sears was absolute. The air scrubbers hummed a low, rhythmic bass note. The rows of server racks stood like monolithic tombstones, black and indifferent.

Alex stood at the Master Console, a glass-topped desk in the middle of the room. He wore a headset. His hand hovered over a physical switch, a heavy, red toggle switch labeled INITIATE.

"Sanjay, status of the grid link?" Alex asked.

"The line is green," Sanjay's voice crackled in his ear. "Apex Energy is pushing 40 megawatts into the corridor. They have no idea it's feeding a fortress."

"Vane is expecting a drain," Maya said. "He thinks we are a mall. He thinks we are just lights and HVAC. He doesn't know about the 'Class A' load requirements."

"He's about to find out," Alex said.

02:00 remaining.

The heat in the room was rising. The banks of lights on the front of the racks were flickering orange, standby mode.

"Core temperature is 68 degrees," Maya reported. "Cooling systems are pressurized."

"Government press conference starting in 60 seconds," JD's voice came through. "Director Kline is at the podium."

Alex watched the screen. The Director stepped up to the microphone. She looked tired but determined.

"Today," she said, "we announce a new era of resilience. The Distributed Recovery Node Initiative begins in Baltimore."

01:00.

"She said it," Alex whispered. "The flag is raised."

"Vane's systems just picked it up," Sanjay said, his voice tight with excitement. "His algorithms are reading the designation. They are trying to correlate the news with the asset data. They are looking at the 'Bankrupt Zombie Mall' file."

"Let them look," Alex said. "They are looking at the map, not the territory."

00:30.

The servers began to whine. The sound of ten thousand cooling fans spinning up to full speed. It was the sound of a waking dragon.

"Load increasing," Maya called out. "15%... 20%..."

The lights on the racks shifted from orange to blue. OPERATIONAL.

The massive power draw began. Alex could hear the transformers outside the building hum under the strain. The grid dipped.

"Apex is reacting," Sanjay yelled. "They see the spike. Vane thinks it's a malfunction. He's sending a kill-order to the substation!"

"He's going to cut the power," Alex said. "He's going to try to crash the boot."

"Not so fast," JD said. "Director Kline just issued the Federal Override. The Strategic Power Reserve is now feeding the line. Vane is locked out. He can't touch the switch."

Alex watched the power meter. It fluctuated, then stabilized. The feed was solid. The Federal line, the "Ghost Grid", was flowing into the building.

"System synchronization," Maya said. "We are live on the Federal backbone. We have access to the DoD networks."

00:05.

The screen in front of Alex showed a massive spinning globe. It pulsed with blue light. Nodes were lighting up all over the world. Washington, London, Tokyo.

The servers were alive. The Wealth Command OS was online.

00:00.

Alex threw the switch.

The room filled with a blinding white light as the status boards turned fully green.

SYSTEM ONLINE. SOVEREIGNTY: ESTABLISHED. CASH FLOW DETECTED: POSITIVE.

Alex took a deep breath. He could feel it in the air. The change. The static of the last three months, the fear, the anxiety, the feeling of being a civilian in a hostile world, dissolved.

The system was running. He wasn't just surviving anymore. He was processing. He was executing.

"Welcome back, Commander," JD's voice whispered.

Alex looked at the screen. The ticker tape of "profits" was scrolling in the corner. It wasn't just numbers anymore. It was fuel. It was ammo.

He picked up the secure phone.

"Sanjay," Alex said. "Call Arthur Vane."

"On it."

"Put him on speaker."

A moment later, Vane's voice filled the room. He sounded breathless. Angry. Confused.

"Rivera? What is happening? My grid is locked out! My substation is showing a 'Federal Command' flag! What did you do?"

Alex smiled. He looked around the glowing cathedral of servers he had built out of nothing but dust and courage.

"We didn't do anything, Arthur," Alex said. "We just booted up."

"We're online," Alex said. "And your bill for the electricity is in the mail."

He hung up.

The OS was running. The command was his.

***

Lesson Learnt:

- Military Doctrine: The Boot Sequence. A military operation doesn't begin when the first shot is fired. It begins when the logistics are in place, the comms are established, and the Rules of Engagement are loaded. Until the system is online, you are vulnerable.

- Financial Doctrine: The "Loading Bar" Lie. The financial industry sells you a narrative of "loading up", saving, deferring, waiting. This is to keep you in a passive state. Wealth is not a destination; it is an Operating State. You must move from "Saving" (Loading) to "Deploying" (Running). You must clear the RAM (liquidate safe assets) to run the new Kernel (Sovereign Strategy). If you stay in the loading bar, you are just a hard drive full of data that never gets used.

Chapter 12: Core Processor: Your Value Algorithm

Location: The Bunker | The Command Center | 09:00 Hours

The silence was gone. The peaceful, low-voltage hum of the previous weeks had been replaced by the relentless roar of a supercomputer trying to solve climate change.

The main screen; a wall-sized display that usually showed strategic maps, was now a waterfall of scrolling data. It looked like the Matrix code, but angrier. Green, red, and amber lines cascaded down at a speed that made the eyes water. It wasn't a dashboard; it was a panic attack in digital form.

"Sanjay!" Maya screamed over the noise, her fingers a blur on her keyboard. "Tell me you didn't just authorize a fifty-million-dollar transfer to a llama farm in the Andes!"

"They aren't llamas!" Sanjay yelled back, holding the phone to his ear with one shoulder while typing with the other hand. "They're Alpacas! And it's not a farm! It's a fiber-optic camouflage project! The llama fur provides the perfect insulation for high-frequency trading cables in the high altitude!"

Alex Rivera stood in the center of the room, staring at the waterfall. He felt a migraine blossoming behind his left eye like a poisonous flower.

It had been three days since the "Boot Sequence."

In seventy-two hours, Alex had become the most famous invisible man in the world. The Baltimore node was online. The Aether Dynamics stock was up 400% after the supply chain crisis he had solved. The short-sellers who had mocked him at the gala were now margin-called out of their penthouses.

And now, the world wanted a piece of him.

The inputs were flooding in.

Request for partnership: Lithium mine in Bolivia. Request for funding: Vertical farming startup in Dubai. Request for merger: A Japanese robotics firm. Request for loan: A former Vice President needing cash for a "bio-security venture."

Every VC in Silicon Valley, every oligarch in Dubai, every opportunistic politician in D.C. was trying to route a connection through the Baltimore node.

The OS was overheating.

"Sanjay, kill the Alpacas!" Alex commanded, using his "Indoor Voice," which was usually reserved for warning people about live grenades.

"We can't kill the Alpacas!" Sanjay argued. "The ROI is 8,000% if the insulation theory holds! It's asymmetric warfare, Alex! We win the fiber war!"

"We are not fighting a fiber war!" Alex shouted. "We don't have a 'Fiber Division'! We don't even have a division for 'Animal Husbandry'!"

He looked at the screen. The CPU usage monitor was hovering in the red zone. 98% LOAD.

"We are drowning in opportunity," Alex muttered.

JD walked out of his office, holding a cup of coffee. He looked at the chaos on the floor, Maya sweating, Sanjay screaming, screens flashing, and shook his head.

"The 'Yes' Trap," JD said calmly.

Alex turned to him. "What?"

"This is what happens to a Commander who wins his first battle," JD said, taking a sip. "He thinks he can conquer the whole world. He accepts every surrender. He tries to garrison every village. He spreads his butter over too much bread."

He walked to the main console and pulled a lever labeled THROTTLE.

The roar of the cooling fans died down slightly. The scrolling data slowed to a readable pace.

"Your Core Processor is corrupted," JD said. "You are running on the default setting."

"Which is?"

"Opportunity Maximization," JD said. "The civilian setting. 'Say yes to everything, because you never know when you'll be hungry again.' It's the mindset of a scavenger."

He tapped Alex on the chest. "You are a Sovereign Commander. You are not a scavenger. You are a predator. And a predator does not chase every squirrel in the forest. He picks the weak elk."

"So I say no?"

"You need a Value Algorithm," JD said. "You need a filter that sits between the world and your brain. A gatekeeper. You have one bullet in the chamber. One trigger pull. You have to make sure you're aiming at the right target."

He pointed to the screen. "Right now, you are trying to shoot every squirrel."

Alex looked at the Alpaca investment request. It was tempting. 8,000% return. It sounded like winning.

But did it fit the Kernel? Did it flow?

"I'm meeting someone at noon," Alex said, rubbing his temples. "His name is Orion. He's a... visionary."

JD raised an eyebrow. "Orion? As in, the guy who tried to put a chip in people's brains to record their dreams?"

"Yeah. That one."

"Good luck," JD said. "The man is a black hole of capital. He eats money and emits hype."

"I need to hear him out, "Alex said. "If the technology works, it changes everything."

"Or," JD said, "it destroys your operating system with Feature Creep."

"Feature Creep?"

"When you try to build a Swiss Army Knife that does everything," JD said, "you end up with a tool that does nothing well."

***

Location: The Float Tank Center | Georgetown | 12:00 Hours

The air inside the floatation center smelled of lavender and Epsom salts. It was quiet. So quiet it made Alex's ears ring.

He was led to a private room. In the center, enclosed by white walls, sat a large tank of water. Inside, floating like a fetus in a womb, was Orion.

Orion was twenty-five. He wore swim trunks and had electrodes attached to his temples. His eyes were closed. He looked like a cyberpunk messiah.

"Mr. Rivera," a technician whispered. "He's in the theta-wave state. We can speak through the comms. The sound travels through the water bone-conductively."

Alex leaned over the tank. "Orion?"

The eyes in the water opened. They were wide, unblinking.

"The Commander," Orion said. His voice sounded like it was coming from inside Alex's own head. "I see the data. The Baltimore Node. It's beautiful. It's a digital nervous system for the continent."

"We're expanding," Alex said. "We're looking for the next infrastructure."

"It's biological," Orion said. "The next step is wetware. Not hardware. We."

He tapped the electrode on his head.

"I have built the Mnemosyne Protocol," Orion said. "Memory crystallization. We can store a human lifetime of knowledge on a sugar-cube sized crystal. We can upload it to the web. You can buy the experience of a surgeon, a pilot, a lover."

Alex stared at him. "That's... science fiction."

"It's science," Orion corrected. "I need the Baltimore node to process the bandwidth. The data density is too high for the standard cloud. I need your sovereignty."

"What's the ask?"

"Ten million dollars," Orion said. "For 20% of the IP. We use your node, we launch next month. We become the Google of memory."

Alex did the math. Ten million for a technology that could replace education. It was the Holy Grail. It was the ultimate asymmetric bet.

"We go to the moon, Alex," Orion whispered, the water rippling as he smiled. "We print the currency of consciousness."

The pitch was perfect. It hit every dopamine receptor Alex had. It was legacy. It was impact. It was Flow.

"I'm in," Alex said. "Send the term sheet."

Orion closed his eyes. "Welcome to the future, Commander."

Alex walked out of the center into the bright, harsh D.C. sunlight. He felt a rush. It was the high of the deal. The addiction to the "Yes."

His phone buzzed. Maya. "Alex, we have a problem. The Aether stock just got a margin call. One of the funds we borrowed from is pulling liquidity. They need the five million back by Friday or they foreclose on the Baltimore substation."

Alex stopped. The high vanished, replaced by the cold plunge of gravity.

The margin call.

He had promised five million to Orion. He needed five million to save the power grid.

He only had ten million in liquid cash.

He couldn't say "Yes" to both.

***

Location: The Bunker | The Algorithm Room | 15:00 Hours

The Bunker was quiet again. The "Yes" high had worn off, leaving the gritty residue of reality.

Alex sat at a table. In front of him were two folders.

Folder A: Orion - Mnemosyne Protocol. The Future. High Risk. Infinite Reward. Folder B: Apex Energy Counter-Strike. The Defense. The Grid. Survival.

Sanjay was pacing. "We can do both, Alex! We can delay Orion. We can issue a bridge note to the lender. We can—"

"We are over-leveraged," Alex said, his voice flat. "If we issue a bridge note, the interest eats the profit. We're just running on a treadmill."

"But the memory crystals!" Sanjay pleaded. "That's the sci-fi stuff! That's the movie deal!"

"That's the Feature Creep," JD said, entering the room. He was carrying a sledgehammer.

Alex looked at the sledgehammer. "What is that for?"

"The Rejection Engine," JD said. He walked to a whiteboard. He wiped it clean.

"Alex, tell me about the 'OODA Loop' from your flying days."

"Observe, Orient, Decide, Act," Alex recited.

"Precisely," JD said. "In a dogfight, the pilot who gets through the loop faster wins. Speed is life."

He drew a circle on the board.

"But what happens if you try to Observe everything?" JD asked. "If you look at the enemy, the ground, the fuel gauge, the wingman, the weather, the radio chatter, the missile warning—?"

Alex knew the answer. "You lock up. You crash."

"Target Fixation," JD said. "Or Sensory Overload."

"Right now," JD continued, "your OS is trying to observe everything. The Alpacas. The Memory Crystals. The Lithium. The AI drones. You are Target Fixated on Opportunity."

He lifted the sledgehammer and slammed it into the whiteboard, cracking the drywall.

"We need a Filter," JD said. "We need a Value Algorithm."

He picked up a marker. He wrote a simple equation on the damaged board.

V = (IMPACT x CERTAINTY) / EFFORT

"Value," JD said, "is equal to Impact times Certainty, divided by Effort."

He pointed to Folder A (Orion). "High Impact. High Certainty? Maybe. But what is the Effort?"

"Huge," Alex admitted. "It's unproven tech. It requires new infrastructure."

"Now," JD pointed to Folder B (The Grid). "Impact? Survival. Certainty? 100%, we own the grid. Effort? Low. We just have to pay the bill."

Alex looked at the folders.

"The Algorithm doesn't care about cool," JD said. "It cares about physics. You are a General, Alex. You are not an R&D lab. You are Logistics."

"But the future..." Sanjay whispered.

"The future is built on the present," JD said sharply. "If you lose the grid now, you have no node for Orion later. You are dead."

He turned to Alex. "This is the hardest decision you will ever make. You have to kill the dream to save the reality."

Alex stared at Folder A. The Memory Crystals. It felt like killing a puppy. It felt like betraying the future.

He looked at Folder B. The Grid. The Apel Energy substation. It felt boring. It felt like maintenance.

He closed his eyes. He thought about the Kernel.

FLOW.

Did the memory crystals create Flow? No. It was a science experiment. It was a lottery ticket.

Did the Grid create Flow? Yes. It was the road. It was the pipe. It was the terrain.

"I need to reject Orion," Alex said.

Sanjay gasped. "But 8,000% return!"

"If we invest in the Crystals," Alex said, opening his eyes, "we become a Venture Capital firm. We become gamblers. We lose the Sovereignty. We become dependent on the next big hit."

He picked up Folder A.

"But if we save the Grid," Alex continued, "we own the road. We are the toll booth. We don't care who drives on it, Orion, Google, the Government. We own the asphalt."

He looked at JD. "The Algorithm is Infrastructure First."

"Kill the Alpacas too," Alex said to Sanjay. "Kill the Bolivia mine. Kill the Dubai farms."

"Everything?" Sanjay asked, horrified.

"Everything except the Grid," Alex said. "We clear the RAM. We focus the thread."

Alex picked up the secure phone. He dialed the number for the margin lender.

"This is Rivera," he said. "Wire the five million to the Apex account. Cancel the foreclosure."

"Where is the transfer coming from, Mr. Rivera?" the lender asked.

"From the Mnemosyne investment," Alex said. "The deal is dead."

He hung up.

He placed Folder A in the shredder. It whirred, chewing up the future, spitting out confetti.

Sanjay looked like he was going to cry. "The dream chips, Alex..."

"They were sugar," Alex said, watching the paper strips fall into the basket. "And we just went on a diet."

The room felt lighter. The "Input Storm" on the screens slowed down.

Maya looked at her monitor. "The CPU load is dropping," she said, surprised. "The system is stabilizing. It's running cool."

"Because we stopped asking it to do everything," JD said. "We told it what to do. One thing. The most important thing."

He looked at Alex.

"The Core Processor isn't about finding the answer," JD said. "It's about rejecting the wrong questions."

Alex looked at the single green light glowing on the console: GRID: SECURED.

He didn't have the Memory Crystals. He didn't have the Alpaca fiber.

But he had the power.

And power was the only thing that turned the lights on.

***

Lesson Learnt:

- Military Doctrine: Target Fixation & The OODA Loop. In a high-speed environment, observing too much data creates a bottleneck. A commander must filter the signal from the noise. Speed kills complexity. You cannot act on every variable; you must prioritize based on the Mission.
- Financial Doctrine: The Rejection Engine (Feature Creep). The most important tool in wealth generation is not the ability to say "Yes" to a good deal; it is the discipline to say "No" to a great deal, that doesn't fit the Kernel. Most wealth is lost not by bad investments, but by "drift", drifting from the core competency

(Logistics/Infrastructure) into exciting but unrelated tangents (Tech, Speculation). Sovereignty requires focus. Opportunity Cost is the hidden tax on the wealthy.

Chapter 13: Memory Allocation

Location: The Iron Room | Private Members Club | 20:00 Hours

The room was paneled in dark mahogany, the kind of wood that had absorbed decades of secrets, cigar smoke, and quiet betrayals. It smelled of wealth and testosterone.

Alex Rivera sat at a small table, staring at a man he had hoped to never see again.

Elias Thorne.

They had graduated from West Point together. They had pinned on their bars together. They had both been Majors, commanding companies in the same dusty provinces. But Thorne had taken a different turn in the road.

When he retired, Thorne didn't buy a fishing boat. He founded Vanguard Capital. A private military contractor... but for money. He didn't kill terrorists; he shorted currencies of developing nations and hired locals to start riots to crash the markets. He was a Mercenary of Finance.

"Alex," Thorne said, pouring a glass of amber whiskey. "You look tired. The Bunker keeping you up?"

"I sleep fine," Alex lied.

Thorne slid the glass across the table. He looked the same, hard eyes, a jawline that could cut glass, a scar running through his eyebrow where a sniper's bullet had kissed him in Tikrit.

"I heard about Baltimore," Thorne said, his voice silky. "The zombie mall. The power grid. You're playing soldier in a banker's world."

"Someone has to."

Thorne smiled. It wasn't a friendly smile. "That's the problem with you, Alex. You're nostalgic. You're trying to apply the Rules of Engagement to a knife fight."

He took a sip of whiskey. "I ran a simulation on you. My quants analyzed your decision matrix. Do you know what they found?"

Alex didn't answer.

"They found a Memory Leak," Thorne said, tapping the table. "Specifically, Kandahar. 2014."

The name hit Alex like a physical blow. The convoy. The IED. The decision to delay, that he had second-guessed every night for a decade.

"You still haven't forgiven yourself," Thorne said quietly. "You're allocating 30% of your processing power to that moment. You're still re-fighting the battle. You're trying to 'fix' the past."

"And that makes me weak?" Alex asked, his voice tight.

"It makes you predictable," Thorne corrected. "It makes you risk-averse. Because deep down, Alex, you think you're a failure. You think you're the guy who froze."

Thorne leaned forward. "I know you, brother. You're terrified of making the wrong call again. So you're building fortresses. You're building walls. You're hiding in the Baltimore mall."

"I'm not hiding."

"You're allocating memory to the wrong sector," Thorne said. "You're keeping the trauma in the RAM. In the active cache. It's slowing you down."

He stood up and dropped a folder on the table.

"I'm shorting the grid," Thorne said. "I'm betting that you choke. I'm betting that when the heat comes, you don't execute the order because you're too busy remembering the last time."

Alex looked at the folder. It was a short position against Apex Energy.

"You're the enemy," Alex said.

"No," Thorne said, putting on his coat. "I'm the garbage collector. I clean up the messes that people like you make when they try to be heroes."

He walked to the door, then paused. "You know what the difference is between us, Alex?"

Alex waited.

"I burned the tapes," Thorne said. "I forgot Kandahar. I forgot the mistakes. I formatted the drive. That's why I'm fast, and you're still stuck in the sand."

Thorne left.

Alex sat alone in the Iron Room. The silence was loud. He looked at the reflection in the window. He looked tired. He looked haunted.

Was Thorne right? Was he trying to save the world in Baltimore just to make up for the convoy?

He touched the scar on his own arm, a piece of shrapnel he kept as a reminder.

Memory Allocation. He wasn't managing it. He was hoarding it.

***

Location: The Bunker | The Server Floor | 03:00 Hours

Alex couldn't sleep. He had gone back to the mall, to the server room. The hum of the machines was usually soothing, but tonight it felt like static.

He stood in front of the main rack, looking at the blinking lights. Green. Green. Green.

Except for one.

At the bottom of the rack, a single red light was blinking. DISK FAULT.

"Sanjay," Alex said into his earpiece. "Why is Sector 7 red?"

Sanjay's voice came back, heavy with sleep. "It's the archive drive, Alex. It's old. It's where we backed up the Aether data from the port. It's got a bad sector. It keeps trying to write to a corrupted block of memory."

"Can you fix it?"

"We can run a defrag," Sanjay mumbled. "But the bad sector... usually, you just quarantine it. You wall it off so the OS doesn't try to use it anymore. If the system tries to read the bad sector, it crashes."

Alex stared at the red light.

It was blinking. Ping. Ping. Ping.

It was trying to remember.

"Quarantine it," Alex said.

"Sure. Copying the data and walling it off."

The red light turned off. A small, blue light came on next to it. QUARANTINED.

"Is that better?" Alex asked.

"The system is faster," Sanjay said. "It stops trying to fix the unfixable. It moves on."

Alex walked out of the server room and up to the main deck. JD was there, sitting in the dark, smoking a pipe.

"You met Thorne," JD said. It wasn't a question.

"He says I'm slow," Alex said, sitting down. "He says I'm holding onto the past."

"Thorne is a psychopath," JD said. "But he understands the mechanics of the machine better than you do."

JD pointed to the dark screen. "Sanjay just walled off a bad sector in the drive. Do you know why computer drives fail?"

"Heat. Mechanical wear."

"And Seek Time," JD said. "The head has to move all over the platter to find the data. If the data is fragmented, the head has to fly back and forth, millions of times a second. It burns out the motor."

He looked at Alex.

"Your brain is a hard drive, Alex. And your files are fragmented. The memory of Kandahar is sitting right next to the memory of what you had for breakfast this morning.

When you try to make a decision about the Grid, your head has to 'seek' the trauma of 2014. It has to load the guilt. It has to run the simulation of the IED."

"It wears out the processor," Alex said.

"Exactly," JD said. "Thorne 'formats the drive.' He deletes the guilt. He killed the prisoners. He burned the village. He doesn't feel anything. So he's fast."

JD tapped the ash from his pipe.

"But Thorne is also an idiot," JD said. "Because he thinks memory is space. He thinks you can just delete things to make room."

"What is it, then?"

"It's Institutional Intelligence," JD said. "Thorne deletes the data, so he makes the same mistakes over and over. He has no scars to remind him where the rocks are."

JD stood up and walked to the whiteboard. He drew a rectangle.

"This is the Cache," JD said. "This is the RAM. This is where the fight happens. It has to be clear. Empty. Fast."

Then he drew a huge circle around the rectangle.

"This is the Hard Drive," JD said. "The Archive. This is where the truth lives."

He tapped the board. "Alex, you aren't allocating your memory correctly. You are trying to keep the convoy in the

RAM. You are trying to 'fix' it while you are trying to trade stocks."

"So what do I do?"

"You Archive it," JD said. "You don't delete it. You don't try to fix it. You encrypt it. You store it in a Read-Only format. You look at it, you learn from it, but you don't try to rewrite the code."

He looked at Alex. "The convoy happened. The sector is corrupted. You can't save those soldiers. But you can save the lesson."

"And the lesson was?" Alex whispered.

"Terrain waits for no one," JD said. "And the only way to honor the dead is to command the living."

Alex closed his eyes. He saw the burning truck in Kandahar. He saw the dust. He felt the heat.

He had spent ten years trying to change the ending of the movie in his head. If I had just gone left. If I had just called the air strike.

But the movie was recorded. It was a file. It was done.

"I need to format the RAM," Alex said. "I need to clear the cache."

"Write a log entry," JD said. "Write the After Action Report. Sign it. File it. And then... reboot."

***

Location: The Apex Energy HQ | The Executive Suite | 09:30 Hours

The next morning, Arthur Vane found himself in a war room. Not a metaphorical one.

Thorne was there. The short-sellers were there. They were watching a screen showing the Baltimore power grid.

The "Kill Order" was ready.

"He's going to freeze," Thorne said, checking his watch. "Rivera is going to see the dip, he's going to remember Kandahar, and he's going to hesitate to buy the dip. He's going to protect his capital."

"He's a coward," Vane spat. "Cut the line."

"Cutting," the technician said.

In the quiet of his own command center at the Baltimore Mall, Alex sat in front of the console. Maya was next to him.

"Grid power dropping," Maya said. "They are cutting the feed."

"Buying the dip," Alex said. His voice was steady. Calm.

"Do you want to increase the bid?" Maya asked. "If we buy high, we lose margin."

"All in," Alex said. "Execute Purchase Order Charlie."

He didn't look at the chart. He didn't look at the red numbers falling like blood.

He looked at a small piece of paper taped to the bottom of his monitor. It was his "Archive Entry."

LOG ENTRY 2014-KANDAHAR: STATUS: CLOSED. LESSON: TERRAIN ANALYSIS TRUMPS TIMELINE. ALLOCATED: SECTOR 9 (READ ONLY).

The red light in his brain, the one that had been blinking for ten years, screaming PANIC, was gone. It was quarantined. It was blue.

The data was archived.

The RAM was clear.

He had 100% of his processing power available for the present.

"Buy," Alex commanded.

The Baltimore node activated its backup batteries. It surged onto the local grid, compensating for the cut instantly.

On Vane's screen, the "Cut" failed. The green line didn't drop. It spiked.

"He's... he's counterattacking!" Vane shouted. "He's buying!"

"He's not hesitating," Thorne whispered, staring at the feed in disbelief. "He's not looking at the past."

Alex watched the numbers climb. He wasn't remembering the burning truck. He was watching the current flow.

He was using the past as a foundation, not a ceiling.

"Margin call triggered," Sanjay's voice cheered in his ear. "Vane is getting liquidated. Thorne is getting his face ripped off."

Alex sat back. He felt... light.

The "Memory Leak" was patched. The system was running at peak efficiency.

He remembered the lesson, but he didn't feel the pain.

And that was the difference between a victim and a Commander.

One has scars. The other has armor.

***

Lesson Learnt:

- Military Doctrine: The After-Action Review (AAR). A mission is not over until the lessons are extracted and filed. Rumination (living in the trauma) is a disorder of processing. It keeps the CPU stuck in a loop. To function, a commander must Archive the experience. The event becomes Read-Only data, usable for intelligence but no longer executable code that crashes the system.

- Financial Doctrine: Strategic Memory Allocation (The Sunk Cost Fallacy vs. Institutional Memory). Most investors suffer from "Memory Leaks", they keep past losses in their "RAM" (active thought), which paralyzes their current decision-making. Others suffer from "Amnesia", they delete the memory and repeat the mistake. The Sovereign Wealth Commander Archives the loss. They encrypt the trauma into a "Hard Drive" of experience. They use the Lesson to navigate the terrain, but they do not let the Emotion of the event occupy the mental bandwidth needed for the current trade. Forgive the past but never forget the data.

Chapter 14: Firewall Configuration

Location: The Rivera Residence | The Kitchen | 06:30 Hours

The smell of burnt toast was usually Alex's least favorite way to start the day, but today, the tart smell of carbonized bread mixed with the scent of fear.

Elena Rivera was standing by the granite island, her knuckles white as she gripped her phone. She was vibrating. It was a subtle frequency, like the hum of a high-voltage line, but Alex had been trained to notice micro-tremors.

"Alex," she said. Her voice was an octave too high. "The bank. The mortgage payment. It bounced."

Alex walked over, placing his briefcase on the floor. "What?"

"I tried to pay the mortgage this morning," Elena said, her eyes wide, staring at the screen. "I logged in. And... and..."

She turned the phone toward him.

It wasn't the banking app. It was a video feed. Grainy, shaky, filmed through what looked like a telephoto lens.

It was Elena. Walking into the bank. Getting coffee. Kissing Alex goodbye yesterday morning.

Across the bottom of the video, scrolling text in bright red letters read: THE RIVERA FAMILY: TARGETED. HE IS DESTROYING YOUR PENSION. PROTECT YOUR FAMILY. LINK: DONATE TO THE TRUTH FUND.

"What is this?" Alex asked, his voice dropping into the cold register of combat stress.

"It's on YouTube," Elena whispered. "It's on Twitter. It's everywhere. Someone hacked the bank's security feed. They got the ATM camera. They got the lobby camera. They... they know who we are, Alex."

She looked up at him, her eyes swimming with tears. "Who are these people? Why are they saying you're destroying pensions?"

Alex took the phone. He watched the video. It looped. Elena smiling. Alex driving the Volvo.

It was invasive. It was violating. It was a weaponization of privacy.

"They are targeting the Home Front," Alex said, handing the phone back. "They are trying to flank me."

"Who?"

"The enemy," Alex said. He walked to the window and peeked through the blinds. The street was quiet. The suburban birds were chirping. It was a veneer of peace.

"They can't attack the Baltimore node," Alex said, thinking aloud. "It's too hardened. It's federal infrastructure. They can't short Aether Dynamics anymore because I hold the controlling stake. So they are attacking the unsecured asset."

"You," Elena said. "Us."

"Psychological warfare," Alex said. He turned back to her. "Elena, listen to me. This is a DDoS attack."

"A what?"

"Distributed Denial of Service," Alex said. "They are flooding the zone with garbage traffic, in this case, fear, public shaming, and digital noise, to shut down our operations. They want you panicked. They want me distracted. They want me to come home and hold your hand instead of fighting the war."

"I am panicked, Alex!" she shouted, slamming the phone onto the counter. "My face is on a conspiracy theory video! The neighbors are going to see it. The PTA moms are going to see it!"

Alex walked over and put his hands on her shoulders. "Good."

"Good?"

"Let them see it," Alex said, his eyes hard. "Fear is a data point, Elena. And right now, we're going to weaponize their fear."

He picked up the phone.

"We aren't hiding," Alex said. "We are configuring the Firewall."

***

Location: The Bunker | The Sandbox | 09:00 Hours

The atmosphere in The Bunker was grim. Sanjay was in a full-blown panic, wearing a hoodie with the hood up, pacing the floor like a caged tiger.

"It's a swarm," Sanjay said, gesturing to the wall of screens which were displaying a hate-storm of social media comments. "They are using botnets. Thousands of them. They are spamming every article about Baltimore, every mention of your name. They are tagging the SEC, the FBI, the FTC."

He pointed to a specific screen. "And someone... someone is phishing Elena. They sent her an email that looked like it was from the school district. It was a tracking link. They are trying to geolocate her."

Alex sat in the command chair. He didn't look at the screens. He was cleaning his pistol. It was a ritual he hadn't done in years, but the muscle memory was comforting. The smell of the gun oil.

"They are trying to find a vector," Alex said, sliding the slide back and forth. Click-clack. "A vulnerability."

"A firewall is a wall," JD said. He was standing in the corner, holding a fire extinguisher. He looked at the red cylinder with intense fascination. "But a static wall always fails eventually. The Romans built Hadrian's Wall. It worked for a while. Then the Saxons just went around it."

JD slammed the fire extinguisher onto the table.

"The Maginot Line," JD continued. "The French built a fortress. The Germans flew over it. A wall assumes the enemy is polite. It assumes the enemy will knock on the front gate."

He looked at Alex. "Who is attacking us, Alex? Is it the German Army? No. It's a pack of violent dogs. They don't use tanks. They use fleas."

"So we build a higher wall?" Sanjay asked.

"No," Alex said. "We build a reactive wall."

He holstered the weapon and stood up. "Sanjay, you know what a honeypot is?"

"A trap," Sanjay said. "A fake server designed to look vulnerable, so hackers waste their time attacking it while you trace them."

"Exactly," Alex said. "We aren't going to hide Elena. We aren't going to scrub the internet. We are going to turn her into a honeypot."

Elena's face appeared on the main screen.

"Her phone," Alex said. "It's the weak point. They are phishing it. So we give them what they want."

Maya spun around in her chair. "Alex, you can't put her at risk. If they geolocate her..."

"They won't geolocate her," Alex said. "They'll geolocate us."

He pulled a small, black device from his pocket. It looked like a cell phone, but the antenna was slightly thicker.

"This is a Signal Spoofer," Alex said. "It mimics Elena's phone signature. It broadcasts her IMEI number, her GPS location, her SIM card ID. But the signal is routed through the Baltimore node."

He placed it on the table.

"We give this device to Elena," Alex said. "She keeps it in her purse. We tell her it's an upgrade. A secure line."

"So when they hack her," Maya said, realizing the plan, "they hack the Spoofer."

"And the Spoofer," Alex said, "leads them here."

He pointed to the floor of The Bunker.

"To the Firewall," JD said, smiling. "The empty fort isn't empty. It's a trap."

"But," Sanjay said, his brow furrowed. "If they hack the Spoofer, they see the data. They know the bank accounts. They know the passwords."

"No," Alex said. "They see a Simulation."

He looked at Maya. "Build the Pot, Maya. A mirror image of our finances. But put the money in the 'Alpaca Fund.' Make the passwords '123456'. Make it look easy."

"And when they take it," Sanjay asked.

"Then we destroy them," Alex said. "Because in the digital world, just like in the physical one, if you enter a hostile territory uninvited, you are subject to the laws of that territory. And our law is lethal."

***

Location: The "Honeypot" (Virtual Space) | 23:00 Hours

The attack came at 11:00 PM.

The streets of the suburb were dark. The Rivera house was silent. Elena was asleep, exhausted by a day of media scrutiny.

Inside The Bunker, the lights were red. Battle Stations.

"They took the bait," Maya whispered. "They accessed the Spoofer."

On the main screen, a map of the world lit up. A line of data was streaming from a residential node in Virginia (the Rivera house) to a server farm in Romania.

"They are downloading the files," Sanjay said, his fingers flying across his keyboard. "They are grabbing the 'routing numbers.' They are grabbing the 'SWIFT codes.'"

Alex watched the progress bar. 45%... 60%...

"Wait," Maya said, her voice sharp. "They aren't just downloading. They are uploading."

"What?"

"They are injecting a worm," Maya said. "They are trying to brick the system. They want to wipe the accounts."

"Let them," Alex said calmly.

"They are in the Pot," JD said, watching the screen like a hawk. "They think they are in the vault. But they are actually in the airlock."

"100% Downloaded," Maya said.

The attackers struck. Suddenly, the data stream reversed. It surged out of the Romanian server and back toward Virginia. They were trying to trigger a wipe command. To delete the files and burn the evidence.

"Execute the Kill Switch," Alex commanded.

Maya tapped a key.

On the screen, the "Virginia" node, the Signal Spoofer, didn't just shut down. It pulsed.

The data that was flowing back from Romania hit the Spoofer. And the Spoofer sent a return packet.

Not a data packet.

A payload.

"The Hunter-Killer Patch," Sanjay whispered, grinning with demonic delight. "It's a piece of code I wrote. It doesn't just destroy the connection. It back-traces the handshake. It burns their IP address. It burns their physical location. And it... it jumps."

"Jumps?"

"It hops into their local network," Sanjay said. "It infects their router. Then their PC. Then their printer. It looks for any open ports and propagates. We aren't just killing the botnet, Alex. We're taking it over."

The screen turned from red to a deep, ominous purple.

"We're inside their system," Maya said. "We have eyes on."

Alex walked to the screen. The map zoomed in. Not on Virginia. On Romania. Then on a proxy server in the Caymans. Then...

McLean, Virginia. Address: 1400 Tysons Blvd. Entity: Apex Energy HQ.

"They aren't using random hackers," Alex said, staring at the address. "It's Vane. It's Thorne. They are doing it from their own building."

"Criminal stupidity," JD said, shaking his head. "They forgot the first rule of assassination. Don't pull the trigger yourself; hire a hitman. Or if you do, wear gloves. They left fingerprints."

Alex looked at the time. 11:15 PM.

"They are asleep," Alex said. "They think they won."

"Elena is safe," Maya said. "The Spoofer is wiped. The bank accounts they saw were fake. The only thing they stole was the virus."

"What do we do with the access?" Sanjay asked. "Do we wipe Apex? Do we turn off their lights?"

"No," Alex said. "That's an act of war. This is an act of defense."

He looked at JD. "What's the doctrine, General?"

"Deception," JD said. "And preparation."

"Lock the data," Alex said. "Archive everything. Every keystroke, every email, every financial transaction they used to fund the attack."

"And then?"

"And then," Alex said, a cold, thin smile touching his lips, "we let them wake up in the morning thinking they won."

He turned to the screen, to the glowing purple node that represented the enemy's breach.

"They have the virus," Alex said. "And the virus has a microphone. From now on, whenever they talk about us, we listen."

He picked up his jacket.

"Where are you going?" Maya asked.

"Home," Alex said. "Elena will wake up in the morning and check her phone. She'll see the news stories. She'll be scared."

He paused at the door.

"But I need to be there to tell her the truth," Alex said. "That the noise is just that. Noise. And we have the ultimate firewall."

"What is that?"

"A conscience," Alex said. "And a back-trace."

He walked out into the night.

The suburb was quiet. The crickets were chirping.

But in the digital ether, the war was silent. And Alex Rivera was holding the silence.

***

Location: The Rivera Residence | Master Bedroom | 07:00 Hours

Sunlight streamed through the curtains. Dust motes danced in the beams.

Elena woke up. She reached for her phone. The habit was ingrained. Check the news. Check the damage.

She expected hate mail. She expected threats.

She saw... nothing.

She refreshed Twitter. Her name was trending, but the stream was... different.

It wasn't hate. It was confusion.

“Wait, the ‘Truth Fund’ account was suspended?” “Why did the video get taken down for copyright violation?” “Did you guys see that glitch? The video turned into an ad for Alpaca wool socks?”

Elena sat up, blinking.

She looked at Alex. He was sitting in the armchair, watching her, holding a cup of coffee.

"What did you do?" she asked.

"I built a wall," Alex said. "But not to keep them out. To keep them in."

"Is it over?"

"It’s never over," Alex said. "But they aren't in the operating system anymore. They’re quarantined. They’re in the sandbox."

He stood up and walked to the window. The neighborhood was waking up. The paperboy was throwing papers. The world was turning.

"Elena," Alex said. "They wanted to make you afraid. They wanted to make us feel unsafe. To make us retreat to the 'Glide Path'."

He turned to her.

"But we are the OS now," Alex said. "We don't retreat. We patch."

Elena looked at her phone. The screen flickered. For a split second, a tiny graphic of a llama wearing sunglasses flashed in the corner.

She laughed. It was a rusty sound, but it was a laugh.

"Did you hack them with llamas?" she asked.

"It was a gift," Alex said, smiling. "From our friends in the Andes."

He walked over and kissed her on the forehead.

"Go make breakfast," Alex said. "I have a war to run."

He walked out, his step light.

The firewall was configured. The perimeter was secure.

And the enemy? The enemy was carrying the bug. And Alex was listening to every word they said.

***

Lesson Learnt:

- Military Doctrine: Defensive Depth & The Honeypot. Static defenses (castle walls) fail against adaptive threats. True defense is layered. You trade space for intelligence. You create an attractive-looking vulnerability (a honeypot) to draw the enemy into a kill zone where you control the terrain.

- Financial Doctrine: The Sovereign Firewall (Identity & Asset Protection). In a digital age, your identity is a financial asset. Public exposure (doxxing) is a tactical weapon designed to disrupt your decision-making (The OODA Loop). The defense is not to hide, but to create a Decoy Identity. Separate your public persona (the honeypot) from your actual assets. Let the enemy attack the shadow; let them steal the fake data. And let the payload they carry back to their own base be your counter-intelligence tool. True safety isn't a wall; it's a trap that destroys the intruder.

Chapter 15: Multi-Thread Execution

Location: The Rivera Residence | The Kitchen | 08:00 Hours

Sunday morning in the Rivera household usually possessed the chaotic, rhythmic energy of a well-organized military convoy. But today, it felt like a traffic jam in Kolkata.

Alex Rivera stood in front of the stove, a spatula in one hand and his secure phone in the other. He was attempting to execute three distinct operations with a brain that was currently running at 99% capacity.

"Flip!" Alex shouted, flipping a pancake.

His phone buzzed. Bitcoin was dipping. A micro-trend line on a 15-second chart was curling downward like a dying fern.

"Dad, help me with this equation!" his son, Ben, yelled from the kitchen table. "If train A leaves Chicago at 4 PM..."

"I'm listening!" Alex said. "Buy the dip." He tapped the phone. Trade Executed.

The pancake landed on the floor with a wet splash.

"Ew," Ben said.

"Mom!" Ben yelled.

The back door opened. Elena walked in, carrying a bag of groceries. She saw the pancake on the floor. She saw Alex staring at his phone with the intensity of a bomb disposal expert. She saw Ben eating dry cereal out of a box.

She stopped. She looked like a sergeant major who had just walked into a latrine that hadn't been cleaned in a month.

"Alex," she said, her voice dangerously calm. "What is happening?"

"I'm multi-tasking," Alex said, scraping the pancake off the floor. "I'm managing the household, the education, and the liquidity position."

"No," Elena said, putting the groceries down on the counter with a heavy thud. "You are buffering. You are a computer with too many windows open, and you're about to freeze."

She walked over to him and gently took the secure phone out of his hand.

"Hey, I was in a trade!"

"The trade will be there," Elena said. "The burnt pancake is a loss we can never recover."

She looked him in the eye. "You're trying to be everything to everyone, Alex. All at the same time. You're trying to be the dad, the trader, the General, the husband. You're single threading your life."

Alex looked at the spatula. She was right. In the military, he had a staff. The Intel officer gave him the data. The Logistics officer moved the fuel. He just made the decision.

Here, he was trying to be the entire Division.

"You're bottlenecking," Elena said. "You need a better operating system."

Alex sighed. He leaned against the counter. "I know. JD says I need to learn how to run multiple threads at once. Without crashing."

"Multi-threading?" Ben asked, his mouth full of Cheerios.

"Doing ten things at the same time," Alex said.

"Like a computer?" Ben asked. "Dad can't even chew gum and walk."

"Out," Elena pointed at Ben. "Shower. Schoolwork. Move."

Ben ran, leaving a trail of cereal dust.

Elena handed Alex back his phone. The pancake was gone. The moment was over.

"Go to your Bunker," she said, kissing him on the cheek. "Figure out how to be a machine. Just come back in one piece."

Alex looked at the blank screen.

"I'm not a machine, El," he said quietly.

"That's the problem," she said. "Machines don't get tired. You do."

He walked out the door, but the lesson stuck. He was running a linear process in a nonlinear world.

***

Location: The Bunker | The Theater Room | 14:00 Hours

The Bunker was configured differently today. Usually, there was one main screen. Today, there were three.

Screen Left: High-frequency currency charts. Lines moving so fast they looked like static. Screen Center: The tactical map of the Baltimore Node and the Apex Energy grid. Screen Right: A long-term portfolio analysis. Slow, boring curves over ten years.

JD stood in the middle, holding a conductor's baton. He was wearing a tuxedo T-shirt.

"Welcome to the Orchestra," JD said. "Today, we learn to conduct a symphony."

Alex sat in the command chair. "I'm listening. Elena says I'm buffering."

"Elena is a wise woman," JD said. "The human brain is a single-core processor. It does one thing at a time. It processes input, then output. It queues the tasks."

He pointed to the screens.

"The market? The market is a supercomputer. It processes billions of tasks simultaneously. If you try to fight it with a single-threaded brain, you lose. You are a musketeer fighting a tank."

Sanjay rolled his chair over. He was wearing three watches on his left arm.

"I'm running three threads right now," Sanjay said proudly. "Thread one: Tracking the price of Alpaca fur in Peru. Thread two: Debugging the honeypot code for Vane. Thread three: Eating a donut."

Maya looked up from her keyboard. "You dropped jelly on the keyboard, Sanjay."

"That's thread four," Sanjay said, licking his finger.

JD ignored them. He pointed to the center screen.

"Alex, traditional financial planning tells you to 'Diversify.' They tell you to buy some stocks, some bonds, some real estate. That is Asset Diversification."

He shook his head. "It's garbage. It's just parking your cars in different garages. They are all still parked."

He walked to the left screen.

"The Sovereign Wealth Commander doesn't diversify assets. He diversifies Time."

"Time?" Alex asked.

"Time Horizons," JD said. "He runs a Multi-Thread Execution. He executes three distinct strategies, operating on three different time clocks, simultaneously."

He tapped the screens in order.

"Thread Alpha: The Sniper (Micro-Seconds). High-frequency scalping. You are not investing. You are providing liquidity to the market. You are skimming the bid-ask spread. You make thousands of small trades a day. It's dangerous. It requires algorithms. It generates Cash Flow."

He moved to the center screen.

"Thread Bravo: The Commander (Months to Years). Strategic positioning. This is your Aether stock. Your Baltimore Node. This is the 'Boot Up Sequence.' You hold these assets for the duration of the campaign. You are fighting the war here. This generates Capital Appreciation."

He moved to the right screen.

"Thread Charlie: The King (Decades). Legacy construction. This is the trust structures, the tax-free endowments, the generational real estate. These assets never move. They are buried deep in the bedrock. They generate Sovereignty."

JD turned to Alex.

"Most investors are single-threaded. They buy a stock and pray it goes up in ten years. If it drops tomorrow, they panic. They are mixing the Time Scales."

He tapped the center of his chest.

"You are going to run all three threads. At the same time. You are going to scalp for cash flow to feed the Strategic Position. You are going to hold the Strategic Position to fund the Legacy. You are creating a perpetual motion machine."

Alex stared at the three screens. It made sense.

"I've been trying to do everything with one pot of money," Alex said.

"Precisely," JD said. "And when you need cash, you sell the long-term asset. You kill the King to feed the Soldier. That is why you never get ahead."

Suddenly, the lights in the Bunker turned red. A siren began to wail, a low, rhythmic whoop.

Maya spun around. "It's starting. The Harvest."

Sanjay sat up, his three watches jingling. "Vane and Thorne are making their move. They are attacking the Apex stock."

On the center screen, the line of Apex Energy began to plummet. It didn't drift down. It fell off a cliff.

"They are shorting it to zero," Sanjay yelled. "They released a fake news report saying the Baltimore Node is leaking radiation!"

"Radiation?" Alex laughed. "It's a server farm!"

"But the algos don't know that!" Maya shouted. "They are selling! The volume is insane! We are losing capital!"

Alex looked at the screens. The panic was here. The single-threaded investors were dumping everything.

"Thread Alpha," Alex commanded. "Engage the Snipers."

Sanjay's hands flew across his keyboard. "I'm buying the dip! I'm scalping the bounce!"

"Thread Bravo," Alex said, his voice like iron. "Execute the Echo Protocol."

"The what?"

"We sell," Alex said. "We sell half our Aether position. We join the panic. We drive the price down further."

"But that loses money!" Maya cried.

"No," Alex said. "It tricks them. It makes them think the collapse is real."

He pointed to the right screen. "Thread Charlie. Prepare the absorption."

JD smiled, tapping his baton against his leg. "The Conductor has arrived."

***

Location: The Trading Floor (Virtual) | The Bunker | 15:00 Hours

The air in The Bunker was no longer just air; it was information. It was pressurized with data.

Alex sat in the center chair. He was no longer a man; he was a fiber-optic nerve ending. He could feel the pulse of the global economy.

It was beating irregularly. Arrhythmia.

"Thread Alpha status," Alex barked.

"Scalpers active!" Sanjay shouted, his eyes locked on the left screen. "We are eating the spread! Every time the price bounces, we buy and sell in the same millisecond! We are generating $50,000 a minute!"

"Keep the fuel flowing," Alex said. "Don't get greedy. Take the pennies. Leave the dollars for Thread Bravo."

"Roger that!"

"Thread Bravo status," Alex said.

"Aether is down 40%," Maya reported. "Margin calls are going out across the board. Vane is covering his shorts. He thinks he's winning."

"Let him think it," Alex said. "Dump the rest. Drop the hammer."

Maya hit a key. SOLD.

On the chart, the line spiked down. Through the floor. Into the basement.

Vane and Thorne were celebrating. They were shorting. They were selling assets they didn't own, betting they could buy them back for pennies. They were stripping the flesh from the carcass of the market.

"They are going for the kill," JD said, watching the Center screen. "They are going to bankrupt Apex. They are going to bankrupt you, Alex."

"They are attacking the wrong thread," Alex said.

He took a deep breath. The hardest part of multi-threading was the dissociation. You had to be three different people at once.

He had to be the terrified trader watching his life savings vanish (Thread Bravo). He had to be the cold robot scalping pennies (Thread Alpha). And he had to be the immortal King buying the rubble (Thread Charlie).

"Thread Charlie," Alex whispered.

"Ready," Maya said. "The debt market is crashing. No one wants Apex bonds. They are yielding 80 cents on the dollar."

"Buy them," Alex said. "Buy them all."

"With what?"

"With the cash from Thread Alpha," Alex said. "And the cash from selling Aether."

He looked at the right screen. The Legacy screen.

"They are selling us the company for pennies," Alex said. "Because they are afraid of the news. But we know the truth."

"Which is?"

"That the Baltimore Node isn't a liability," Alex said. "It's the only thing that matters."

On the left screen, Sanjay's scalpers were humming. A river of nickels was flowing into the account. On the center screen, the Aether stock was hitting zero. On the right screen, the debt of Apex Energy was being bought by Alex at junk prices.

"He's trapped," JD said, pointing to a ticker of Thorne's fund. "Thorne shorted so much that he can't cover. He needs the stock to stay at zero."

"Buy the last block," Alex commanded.

Maya typed. EXECUTED.

The screen flashed green. DEBT POSITION: ACQUIRED.

"What now?" Sanjay asked. "We have a mountain of junk bonds and a stock that's worth zero."

"Now," Alex said, checking his watch, "We flip the switch."

He picked up the red secure phone. The direct line to the Department of Energy.

"This is Rivera," he said. "Execute the Press Release."

On the screen, a news feed popped up. PRESS RELEASE: DEPARTMENT OF ENERGY CONFIRMS BALTIMORE NODE AS CRITICAL INFRASTRUCTURE. POWER GRID SECURED.

The room went quiet.

For three seconds, nothing happened. The algos were reading. The humans were reading.

Then, the market realized, it had been lied to.

The radiation story was fake. The Baltimore Node was online. Apex Energy was not bankrupt; it was the backbone of the Eastern Seaboard.

Thread Alpha started screaming. "It's spiking!" Sanjay yelled. "The bots are buying back! They are panic-buying!"

Thread Bravo reversed. The Aether stock, which had been at $5, shot up. $10. $20. $50.

But Thread Charlie...

That was where the magic happened.

Alex owned the debt. The bonds.

And the bonds were convertible.

As the stock price of Apex hit $50, the bonds, worth pennies an hour ago, became worth gold.

"Thorne," JD said, laughing softly. "He shorted the stock at $50. He has to buy it back at $50 to cover his bet."

"But we own the company," Alex said. "We own the debt. We call the loan."

"You're forcing him to buy the company from himself?" Maya asked, her eyes wide.

"I'm forcing him to buy his freedom," Alex corrected. "And the price is everything he has."

He watched the screen of Thorne's fund. It was flashing red. LIQUIDATION EVENT.

"Thread Alpha is the muscle," Alex said, watching the numbers fly. "Thread Bravo is the weapon. But Thread Charlie..."

He looked at the Legacy screen. The debt was now worth ten times what he paid for it.

"Thread Charlie is the castle," Alex finished. "We just bought the grid for the price of a used Honda."

Sanjay stopped typing. He stared at the screen.

"We just..." Sanjay whispered. "We just ate a hedge fund."

Alex sat back. He didn't feel tired. He didn't feel like he was buffering anymore.

He felt like he was everywhere at once.

He was the scalper. The trader. The King.

His phone buzzed. A text from Elena. "Pancakes are burnt. The market is crazy. Are you okay?"

Alex smiled. He typed back. "I'm running on all cylinders, El. And we won."

He looked at JD. "The OS is stable."

"The threads are synched," JD said. "You are no longer a linear processor, Alex. You are the Conductor."

The lights in the Bunker turned from red to a soft, victorious blue.

The Harvest was over. And Alex Rivera hadn't just survived it. He had reaped it.

He had taken their fear, processed it, and sold it back to them as profit.

***

Lesson Learnt:

- Military Doctrine: Multi-Domain Operations. Modern warfare isn't just ground troops. It's air, cyber, space, and info, all happening at the same time. A Commander must manage disparate threads, the kinetic battle, the diplomatic pressure, the logistical supply, simultaneously. Victory goes to the side that can integrate these threads into a cohesive strategy.

- Financial Doctrine: Multi-Thread Execution (Time-Diversification). The flaw of traditional investing is the mixing of Time Horizons. Do not mix your grocery money (Thread Alpha) with your retirement money (Thread Bravo) or your legacy money (Thread Charlie).

- Thread Alpha (Scalping): High frequency, low risk per trade. Generates immediate cash flow to fund the operation.
- Thread Bravo (Strategic): Medium term. The core campaign. High risk/reward, but funded by Alpha.
- Thread Charlie (Legacy): Long term. Deep value. Generational assets that never move but provide the bedrock.

The Insight: When the market crashes, Alpha provides liquidity to survive. Bravo provides the volatility to profit. Charlie provides the "buy low" opportunity that locks in generational wealth. You win on all timelines simultaneously.

Part IV: The Campaign

(The Live Fire Test)

Chapter 16: Home Territory Defense

Location: The Rivera Residence | 20:00 Hours

The smell of victory was distinct. It wasn't sweat, or cordite, or ozone. It smelled of slow-roasted prime rib, garlic butter, and a very expensive bottle of Cabernet that had been breathing for an hour.

Alex Rivera stood in his dining room, holding a crystal glass filled with liquid garnet. The room was shining in the warm, golden light of the chandelier, reflecting off the faces of the people he loved.

Elena was laughing at something Ben said. Sarah was actually looking up from her phone, smiling. The dog, Barnaby, a Golden Retriever who shed enough fur to knit a sweater every week, was asleep on Alex's foot.

It was perfect. It was the "Peace Dividend." The very thing he had been running from, for three months.

"To the Commander," Elena said, raising her glass. Her cheeks were flushed. "And to the end of the stress."

"To the future," Ben corrected, raising his soda. "Are we rich now, Dad? Like, Iron Man rich?"

Alex looked at his son. He thought of the bank account. The multi-thread execution had worked. Thread Alpha (the scalping) was still humming, feeding cash into the system. Thread Bravo (Aether/Apex) had stabilized after the squeeze, now sitting pretty at an amazing valuation. Thread Charlie (The Debt) was the crown jewel; he owned the grid.

Technically, yes. They were rich. But looking at Ben's expectant face, Alex felt a strange hollowness in his chest.

"We are... comfortable," Alex said carefully.

"Comfortable?" Elena laughed. "Alex, you just took down a hedge fund and a power company in the same afternoon. I think you can upgrade from 'comfortable' to obnoxious."

"I bought a boat," Alex admitted. "Not a big one. But a boat."

The kids cheered. Even Sarah looked impressed.

"And," Alex continued, feeling a rush of dopamine that was better than any combat adrenaline, "I paid off the mortgage."

The room went silent.

"You paid it off?" Elena whispered. "The whole thing?"

"Every penny," Alex said. "The bank has no lien on this house. We own the roof. We own the dirt."

Elena put her glass down. She stood up and walked around the table. She wrapped her arms around his neck and hugged him tight.

"It's over," she whispered into his ear. "The grind. The worry. We're safe."

Alex hugged her back. He smelled her shampoo. Lavender and safety.

He wanted to believe it. He wanted to believe that the war was over and he could just be a guy with a boat and a mortgage-free deed.

But deep in the Commander's cortex, the part of his brain that never slept, he knew the truth.

Victory wasn't the end of the war. It was just the moment you became the biggest target on the board.

The enemy hadn't surrendered. They were just regrouping.

***

Location: The Rivera Residence | The Front Porch | 22:30 Hours

The dishes were done. The kids were in bed. The house was settling into its nighttime creaks and groans.

Alex sat on the porch swing, a cigar between his fingers, he didn't smoke it, just chewed the end, and watched the moths batter against the porch light.

The neighborhood was quiet. The American Dream.

JD Donovan walked out of the shadows of the driveway. He wasn't wearing his usual Bunker gear. He was wearing a suit that looked like it cost more than Alex's first house. He looked like a CEO. Or a hitman.

"Nice party," JD said, sitting on the swing next to him. "The Cabernet was excellent. 2012? Good year."

"It was," Alex said. "We won, JD. It's done."

JD didn't look at him. He looked at the street. The darkness between the streetlights.

"You paid off the mortgage," JD said.

"Yes."

"You put the boat in your name."

"Yes."

"You transferred the Aether shares to your personal brokerage account."

Alex stopped chewing the cigar. "What are you getting at, General?"

JD turned to him. In the dim light, his face looked like a skull.

"You just painted a giant target on your wife's forehead, Alex," JD said softly.

"What?"

"The mortgage is gone," JD said. "You own the house outright. That means your name is on the deed. A public record. You transferred the Aether shares to your personal account. That means your name is on the DTC list."

He stood up and walked to the railing.

"The enemy can't fight you in the market anymore, Alex. You kicked them out of the exchange. You own the pipe. You own the grid. So where do they fight you?"

JD turned back.

"They fight you here," he said, pointing at the house. "They fight you in the Courts. They fight you in the Tax Code. They fight you in the Civil Courts."

Alex felt a cold trickle of sweat run down his spine.

"They can't beat your algorithm," JD continued. "So they will beat your process. They will sue you. They will lien you. They will subpoena you. They will use the Law as a blunt instrument until you bleed to death."

"They can't sue me for winning," Alex said, his voice hard.

"They can sue you for anything," JD said. "Thorne is alive. Vane is alive. They have lawyers. Thousands of them. They don't charge by the hour; they charge by the pound of flesh they can strip from the bone."

Alex looked at the house. The windows glowed with warm yellow light. Sarah's room. Ben's room.

"They would attack the house?" Alex asked. "Elena?"

"They aren't monsters, Alex," JD said. "They are accountants. To them, this house isn't a home. It's a ledger entry with a negative balance. They will zero it out."

"You're paranoid," Alex said, standing up. "It's over."

"The Peace Dividend," JD said, shaking his head. "It's the most dangerous drug in the world, Alex. It makes you lower your shield."

He walked down the steps.

"Get some sleep," JD said over his shoulder. "Tomorrow, the Home Front war begins."

***

Location: The Rivera Residence | The Driveway | 08:00 Hours

Monday morning arrived with the brightness of a headache.

Alex was walking to his car, coffee in hand, tie slightly loose. He was late. He had a meeting with the new board of Apex Energy to officially dissolve the old management and install the Sovereign OS.

He opened the car door.

Then he heard the sound.

It wasn't a gunshot. It was the sound of a heavy diesel engine braking. The hiss of air brakes.

Alex turned.

Two black SUVs were idling at the end of the driveway. They were discreet. No lights. No markings. Just black steel and tinted glass.

Four men got out. They weren't wearing tactical gear. They were wearing suits.

Not good suits. Off-the-rack suits. Suits that looked like they had been slept in.

The lead man held a clipboard. He looked tired. He looked like a meter-maid.

"Alex Rivera?" the man asked.

Alex's hand went to his hip, out of habit, but his phone was there, not his pistol.

"Who's asking?"

"My name is Miller," the man said. "I'm a Process Server for the District of Columbia. And this is Mrs. Gable from the Department of Revenue."

He pointed to the house.

"We have a Civil Asset Forfeiture Order," Miller said. "And a Tax Lien for unpaid capital gains dating back to the incorporation of Aether Dynamics."

Alex froze. "Capital gains? I haven't sold anything."

"It's a Constructive Receipt claim," Miller said, bored. "The IRS contends that the acquisition of Apex Energy stock constitutes a taxable event based on the fair market value of the infrastructure assets acquired."

"That's insane," Alex said. "That's not tax law."

"It is," Miller said, shrugging. "If a judge signs it. And we have a judge who will sign it by noon."

He handed Alex a stack of papers. It was thick enough to stop a tank round.

"Also," Miller continued, "Mr. Thorne has filed a civil suit alleging Ricochet violations. He claims you manipulated the market to bankrupt him. That puts a freeze on all your personal assets."

The house door opened.

Elena stood there, wearing her bathrobe, holding a coffee mug. She saw the SUVs. She saw the papers.

"Alex?" she asked. "Who is it?"

"It's nothing, El," Alex said, his eyes locked on Miller. "Just a bureaucratic misunderstanding."

"It's not a misunderstanding," Miller said, his voice hardening slightly. "Mr. Rivera, if you don't sign the Acknowledgment of Service, we will have to place a physical levy on the property."

"A what?"

"Seize the assets," Miller said. "The cars. The boat. The art inside. We have a writ."

Elena walked down the steps. "You can't take our car. It's for the kids."

"It's not your car, Ma'am," Miller said, not unkindly. "It's a liquid asset attached to a delinquent account. It's just numbers."

Alex stepped between Miller and Elena.

"Leave," Alex said. The Command Voice.

"Mr. Rivera," Miller sighed, "I'm just a guy with a clipboard. I'm not the enemy. If you force me to leave, I come back with the Sheriff. And he brings deputies. And they bring guns."

Miller looked at his watch. "The lien hits at noon. If you don't bond the debt, twenty million dollars, the Sheriff starts removing furniture at 1:00 PM."

He put a card on the hood of Alex's car.

"Hire a good lawyer, Mr. Rivera. You're going to need one."

The SUVs drove away.

Alex stood in the driveway. The air felt heavy. The sun was shining, the birds were chirping, and the "Peace Dividend" was dead.

Elena touched his arm. "Alex, what did you do?"

Alex looked at the house. The home. The sanctuary. He realized he had left the gates open.

He had fought a war in the cloud, in the markets, on the fiber lines. But he had forgotten the oldest rule of warfare.

Protect your Supply Lines.

***

Location: The Bunker | The War Room | 10:00 Hours

Alex slammed the door of The Bunker. He didn't sit. He paced. He was vibrating with a rage, he hadn't felt since Kandahar.

"They can't do this," Alex shouted. "It's thuggery. It's state-sponsored theft!"

Sanjay was at his station, typing furiously. "It's worse than theft, Alex. It's a Systemic Kill."

He turned the screen. It showed a diagram.

"Look," Sanjay said. "The Lien attaches to your Name. Your Name is the Entity. Your Name owns the House. Your Name owns the Stocks. Your Name is the glitch."

"They are weaponizing the law," JD said. He was sitting in the corner, carving a piece of wood into the shape of a shield.

"The Courts," JD said, spitting wood shavings, "are just another battlefield, Alex. It's slow terrain. It's muddy. But the physics are the same."

He stood up. "You are trying to fight a tank with a rifle. You are trying to argue 'Fairness' in a system designed for extraction."

"So I pay the bond?" Alex asked, his voice tight. "I give them twenty million?"

"Then they file another suit," Maya said from her screens. "Then another. They will bleed you dry, Alex. Thorne has billions. He can litigate you forever. He doesn't need to win the case; he just needs to keep you in the courtroom."

Alex stopped pacing. "So I lose the house."

"No," JD said sharply. "You abandon the house."

"What?"

"You think the house is the bricks?" JD asked. "You think the home is the address? No. The Home is the people. The Territory is the Sovereignty."

He walked to the whiteboard. He drew a square.

"This is your current setup," JD said. He drew a stick figure of Alex, a stick figure of Elena, the house, the stocks. All inside the square.

"You are one entity," JD said. "The Riveras. A soft target. A single point of failure."

He erased the drawing. He drew a circle around the square. Then he drew a line from the square to the circle, breaking through it.

"You need to pierce the veil," JD said. "You need to separate the People from the Assets."

"I don't understand," Alex said.

"Elena Rivera is a civilian," JD said. "She is a non-combatant. But you are treating her like a soldier in your army. You are putting her name on the front line."

He tapped the board.

"The Trust," JD said. "The Family Trust."

"I have a trust," Alex said. "For the kids."

"Not a trust," JD said. "A Sovereign Entity."

He looked at Maya. "Pull up the documents for the 'Black Knight' protocol."

Maya typed. A new set of legal forms appeared on the screen.

"This is a complex structure," Maya said. "It involves a Cayman Holding Company, an LLC based in Delaware, and a Family Limited Partnership based in Wyoming."

"The Wyoming part," Sanjay interjected, "is the magic. Wyoming has the strongest asset protection laws in the country. Charging orders don't pierce the veil there."

"What does that mean?" Alex asked.

"It means," JD said, "that if you own the house, they can take the house. If the Trust owns the house, and the Trust owes a debt to a Cayman shell company... the house is just an empty box on paper."

Alex stared at the screen. It was a maze of arrows and boxes. It looked like a hydra.

"It's a Ghost House," Alex said.

"It's a Sovereign Territory," JD corrected. "Listen to me. We execute the Transfer. We move the Deed of the House to the Trust. We move the Brokerage Account to the Trust. We move the Boat, the Cars, the Art."

He pointed to Alex.

"You are no longer the owner, Alex. You are the Beneficiary. You are the Commander. But you possess nothing."

"And what about Elena?"

"Elena is the Beneficiary of the Residential License," Maya said. "She gets to live there. She pays the Trust $1 a month in rent. The Trust pays the taxes."

Alex looked at JD. "If I own nothing, they can't lien me?"

"They can lien the Trust," JD said. "But the Trust has no assets on paper. It only has debts. To the other debts. It's a black hole."

JD smiled. "Try to get water from a stone, Mr. Miller."

"So," Alex said slowly, "I surrender ownership to save control."

"Exactly," JD said. "The Home Territory Defense isn't about walls. It's about jurisdiction. You move the flag to a piece of ground they don't have a map for."

"And the twenty million bond?"

"Let them issue it to Alex Rivera," JD said. "Alex Rivera is broke. He has no assets. He has a very nice rental agreement with a Trust in the Caymans."

Alex looked at the diagram. It was brilliant. It was terrifying.

"We have to act fast," Alex said. "Before 1:00 PM."

Sanjay cracked his knuckles. "I just need your biometric signature. I can file the incorporation in Wyoming instantly. I can record the deed transfer in... twenty minutes."

"Do it," Alex said.

"Alex," Maya asked. "Are you sure? You're legally divorcing your assets. If Elena ever leaves you..."

"She's not leaving me," Alex said. "Because I'm not putting her in the crosshairs anymore."

He put his thumb on the scanner.

TRANSFER INITIATED. ENTITY: BLACK KNIGHT HOLDINGS. STATUS: SOVEREIGN.

***

Location: The Rivera Residence | The Driveway | 12:45 Hours

The SUVs returned at 12:50 PM.

The sun was high. The neighborhood was quiet. Kids were getting off the school bus down the street, unaware that a legal siege was happening.

Miller stepped out of the lead car. He had the same clipboard. He looked bored.

"Mr. Rivera," Miller said. "Time is up. We have the writ. We're here to secure the vehicle."

Alex stood in the driveway. He was wearing a suit. He looked calm. He looked like a man waiting for a taxi.

He handed Miller a piece of paper.

"What is this?" Miller asked.

"It's a Bill of Sale," Alex said. "I sold the car this morning."

Miller blinked. "You sold the Volvo?"

"To a private buyer," Alex said. "Cash transaction. I don't own it anymore."

Miller frowned. He looked at his clipboard. "What about the boat?"

"Sold it too," Alex said. "Sorry."

"And the house?"

Alex looked at the house. The yellow light in the windows. The Home.

"I don't own the house," Alex said truthfully. "I'm just the tenant."

Miller stared at him. He looked at the house, then back at Alex. He knew something was wrong. He could smell it. But he was a process server. He wasn't a detective.

"If you don't own the assets," Miller said, "I can't levy them."

"Correct," Alex said. "And since I have no assets, I can't bond the twenty-million-dollar tax lien."

Miller sighed. He took off his glasses and rubbed his eyes. "Mr. Rivera, the State is going to be very unhappy with you."

"I'm very unhappy with the State," Alex said. "But the feeling is mutual."

Miller looked at his watch. He looked at his deputies.

"Pack it up," Miller said. "There's nothing here."

The SUVs drove away.

Alex stood alone in the driveway. The silence returned.

The front door opened. Elena walked out. She looked terrified. She had been watching from the window.

"What happened?" she asked. "Did they take the car?"

"They took the order," Alex said. "They didn't take the car."

He walked up the steps and took her hands.

"El," Alex said. "Do you trust me?"

"With my life," she said.

"Then don't read the mail for a few weeks," Alex said. "And if anyone asks... you rent this place from a corporation in the Cayman Islands."

Elena looked at him, confusion warring with relief. "Alex, what did you do?"

"I built a fortress," Alex said. "But I didn't use bricks."

He hugged her.

"We're safe, El," he whispered. "The House is just a house now. It's not a target anymore."

He looked over her shoulder at the house.

To the world, to the tax man, to the lawyers of Thorne and Vane... the Rivera Residence no longer existed. It was just a data point on a spreadsheet owned by a ghost in the Caribbean.

But to Alex? To Alex, it was finally a Home.

Because for the first time in his life, he had secured the perimeter.

The Defense was complete.

***

Lesson Learnt:

- Military Doctrine: The Perimeter Defense & Decoy Assets. In modern warfare, you cannot defend every asset. You must separate the High Value Targets (your family/flag) from the Decoys (the paper assets). You create a "Ghost Army", legal entities that look like the enemy but are empty shells. The enemy attacks the decoy, wasting ammunition and time on a target that doesn't exist.

- Financial Doctrine: Piercing the Corporate Veil (The Trust Structure). The greatest vulnerability of the wealthy is Public Ownership. Owning assets in your personal name is fighting a tank with a pistol. The Sovereign Defense involves:

  1. The "Alaska" Trust: An irrevocable trust that removes legal ownership from the individual while retaining beneficial use.

  2. The "Wyoming" LLC: A jurisdictional firewall (charging order protection) that makes the entity invisible to civil courts.

  3. The "Cayman" Holdco: An offshore vector that isolates the "Flag" from the domestic tax regime legally.

The Insight: You don't fight the law; you navigate it. You make yourself a "Pauper" on paper and a "King" in reality. The house is not an asset to be seized; it is a residence licensed to a Trust. Sovereignty is the ability to say "I possess nothing" while standing in the middle of your castle.

Chapter 17: Expeditionary Ventures

Location: The Bunker | The War Room | 06:00 Hours

The map on the main screen was no longer displaying stock tickers or shipping lanes. It was displaying a heat map. But not financial heat.

It was thermal heat. And kinetic heat.

A deep, angry red blob occupied the center of the African continent. The Democratic Republic of Kivu. A nation that had been written off by the geopolitical analysts as a "failed state with valuable dirt."

Alex stood in front of the map wearing a tactical vest over his polo shirt. He looked ridiculous, He felt like a father playing soldier, but the heavy Kevlar kept him grounded

"Sixty percent of the world's Cobalt," JD said, tapping the red blob. "It's in that red zone. The stuff that makes your batteries in Baltimore work. The stuff that powers the phones, the EVs, the drones."

"And it's offline," Sanjay said, fanning himself with a clipboard. "The mines are flooded. The rail lines are cut by rebels. The Chinese Belt-and-Road initiative pulled out three weeks ago. The French Peacekeepers are huddled in the capital."

JD turned to Alex. "The market is pricing in a Cobalt shortage for the next five years. If you own the supply, you own the future."

"I own the Baltimore node," Alex said. "I need the Cobalt to keep it running."

"Precisely," JD said. "But you can't buy Cobalt on the open market. There is no market. There is only dirt and blood."

"So, I buy the mine?"

"You buy the Logistics," JD corrected. "You don't dig the hole. You secure the road out of the hole."

He handed Alex a dossier. PROJECT RED DUST.

"The mine is called Le Roi du Sang; The King of the Blood," JD said. "It's currently held by a General named Sika. A warlord who likes Prada suits and machetes. He is preparing to nationalize the mine and kick the workers out."

"Standard resource nationalism," Alex said, opening the file. It showed satellite photos of a compound high in the green hills. Guard towers. Technicals.

"Standard," JD agreed. "Except Sika is smart. He knows he can't run a mine. He doesn't have the engineers. He wants to sell the ore, but he wants to control the flow."

He looked Alex in the eye. "We are going to Kivu. Not to conquer. To partner."

"This is an Expeditionary Venture," Alex said, closing the file. "We leave the Home Territory. We go into the gray zone."

"And we take the flag of the corporation with us," JD said. "We go as a Sovereign Entity. A private nation-state."

Sanjay groaned. "I packed shorts. And bug spray. Lots of bug spray. Did I mention the malaria prophylaxis? I have to take them with grapefruit juice or I vomit."

"Focus, Sanjay," Alex said, checking the chamber of his sidearm. He wasn't taking a rifle, he was a logistics officer, not a sniper, but he carried the authority of a man who knew how to use one.

"We aren't going there to shoot," Alex said. "We are going there to trade. We are going to trade Capability for Commodity."

"What capability?" Sanjay asked. "We teaching them to code?"

"We are teaching them Order," Alex said. "We are going to build a Forward Operating Base for capital."

***

Location: Forward Operating Base "Alpha" | Kivu Border Highlands | 14:00 Hours

The helicopter ride had been an assault on the senses. The heat of the jungle rose up to meet them like a physical blow. The air smelled of damp earth, decay, and diesel fuel.

They landed in a cleared zone, a dusty soccer field that had been converted into a landing pad by a team of contractors who had arrived two days prior.

Alex stepped out, the rotor wash flattening the tall grass. He adjusted his sunglasses. The sun was a hammer.

Waiting for them were two technicals in full battle rattle, and a man in a white linen suit who sat in a plastic chair under a tarp, sipping tea.

General Sika.

He didn't look like a monster. He looked like a mid-level banker who had taken a wrong turn and decided to own the road. He was lean, refined, with eyes that had seen things, that would make a horror writer blush.

"Mr. Rivera," Sika said, in English that was accented with a Parisian polish. "You are late. My patience is... limited."

"Traffic," Alex said, walking up. "Rebels blew a bridge on the supply route."

Sika smiled. It was a shark's smile. "And yet you are here. That implies you have a bridge of your own."

He gestured to the chair opposite him. "Sit. My men are nervous. They say you are CIA. They say you are American Imperialism."

"I'm a businessman," Alex said, sitting. Sanjay stood behind him, sweating profusely, swatting a fly, that seemed to crawl into his ear.

"Businessmen usually send lawyers," Sika said. "They send emails. They do not come in a bird that has armor plating."

"I'm not a lawyer," Alex said. "I'm a Commander."

Sika leaned forward. The air crackled with tension. The technicals fingered their triggers.

"My soldiers," Sika said, waving a hand at the jungle, "they want to eat your liver. They think you are here to steal their King's Blood."

"The Cobalt?"

"The metal," Sika corrected. "It is the blood of the earth. It is cursed. Whoever touches it, dies."

"Then why keep it?" Alex asked.

"Because," Sika said softly, "the world is addicted to the curse. And addiction pays."

He snapped his fingers. A soldier brought a metal box. Sika opened it. Inside sat a raw, jagged chunk of ore. Deep, industrial purple-gray.

"I have ten thousand tons of this," Sika said. "The mine is flooded. The pumps are broken. I need equipment. I need engineers. I need... order."

"I can give you the order," Alex said. "I can bring in the engineers. I can fix the pumps. I can secure the road to the coast."

"And in exchange?" Sika asked, his eyes hard flint.

"I don't want the mine," Alex said. "I don't want the land. I don't want the curse."

He leaned in.

"I want the Flow. I want a contract. 50% of the output goes to me. At market price. Indexed to the Baltimore Spot Rate."

Sika laughed. It was a genuine, surprised sound. "You want a tribute? I am a General! I am a warlord! You ask me to be a toll collector?"

"I ask you to be a Sovereign Partner," Alex corrected. "General, look at the map. You are here. The ocean is there." He pointed to the west. "You are landlocked. You have the product, but no door. The world blockades you. The UN sanctions you."

"I fight them."

"You bleed for it," Alex said. "I open the door. I have the ships. I have the cargo planes. I have the diplomatic immunity that a neutral flag provides."

Alex placed a card on the table. It wasn't a credit card. It was the logo of Black Knight Holdings.

"I own the port in Baltimore," Alex said. "I own the airfield in the Caymans. I can make your Cobalt appear in New York like it was mined in Pennsylvania. I can wash it. I can insure it. I can sell it."

Sika looked at the logo. He looked at the Cobalt. He looked at the sweat on Sanjay's forehead.

"You want to be the launderer," Sika said.

"I want to be the Logistics Provider," Alex said. "You keep the dirt. You keep the power. You keep the flag. I just want to move the product. You become the mine. I become the road."

Sika stared at him for a long minute. The jungle hummed with insects.

"The Chinese," Sika said quietly. "They offered me tanks. They offered me fighters."

"Tanks don't eat," Alex said. "Economies eat. Your people need food. They need medicine. My contract... it comes with a side order."

"What side order?"

"Infrastructure," Alex said. "We don't just fix the mine pumps, General. We pave the road to the village. We upgrade the radio tower. We build a clinic."

Sika's eyes narrowed. "Why?"

"Because efficient roads mean my trucks get stuck less," Alex said. "Healthy workers mean the mine doesn't shut down from cholera. This isn't charity, General. It's Asset Optimization."

He stood up.

"You sell me the blood," Alex said. "I sell you the life. Do we have a deal?"

Sika stood up slowly. He was tall. He loomed over Alex.

"You are a strange American," Sika said. "You do not point a gun at my head. You point a spreadsheet."

"Spreadsheets kill more people," Alex said. "Eventually."

Sika held out his hand. It was hardened, scarred.

"We have a deal," Sika said. "50%. But you fix the pumps by Friday. Or I feed you to the crocodiles."

"Done," Alex said.

***

Location: The Airhead | 18:30 Hours

The loading of the first batch was a chaotic ballet. Russian cargo planes, refitted to carry pallets instead of troops, sat on the tarmac like giant, sleeping beasts.

Sanjay was supervising the weighing of the pallets, shouting at a Kivu sergeant who was trying to load a goat onto the plane alongside the Cobalt.

"No goats! No goats! The goat is not a shareholder!" Sanjay yelled.

Alex stood by the flight line, coordinating with Maya over the radio.

"Maya, what is the satellite overflight?"

"Clear for three hours," Maya's voice said in his ear. "But Alex... I'm picking up a signature."

Alex froze. "What kind?"

"Drone swarm. Generic quad-copters. Not military grade. But they are massing on the northern ridge."

"Vane," Alex said. "He can't kill the deal, so he's going to kill the shipment."

"He hired mercs," Maya said. "Local thugs with tech. They are coming in hot. ETA four minutes."

Alex looked at the cargo planes. They were heavy. laden. They couldn't take off for another twenty minutes.

If the drones hit the fuel bladders, the Cobalt goes up in smoke. The deal with Sika dies. The Baltimore node starves. The Sovereign OS crashes.

"Sanjay!" Alex shouted.

Sanjay looked up, the goat still struggling under his arm. "Yeah?"

"Get the goat off the plane! Deploy the Peacocks!"

Sanjay dropped the goat. It moaned furiously and ran for the jungle. He ran to a shipping container marked "Humanitarian Aid" and ripped the doors open.

Inside weren't medicines. They were automated sentry guns. The "Peacocks."

Alex ran to the central console of the airfield—a rusted tower he had rigged with a server uplink.

"Maya, give me fire control!"

"Link established," Maya said.

On the screen, Alex saw them. Red dots swarming over the northern ridge. Like angry hornets.

He didn't have missiles. He didn't have AAA batteries.

But he had code.

In Chapter 11, during the "Boot Sequence," they had installed a localized defense grid for the Baltimore node. Maya had shipped a portable version of the software, a "Cyber-Sentry" kit.

"Activating Protocol: Dragon's Breath," Alex said.

He typed a command.

The sentry guns on the ground didn't aim up. They aimed... sideways.

"What are you doing?" Maya asked. "They are coming from the north!"

"I know," Alex said. "Hack their navigation."

In the drone cloud control systems, likely run by cheap tablets in a command truck somewhere, the logic suddenly bent. The GPS coordinates didn't show the airfield. They showed the airfield... two miles to the east.

In the swamp.

The swarm banked hard.

"They're going to miss the runway," Sanjay yelled, watching the screen. "They're going to dive into the mud!"

"Not yet," Alex said. "They'll realize the error. They'll correct."

He typed again.

"Initiate Confetti."

In the sky above the swamp, the drones suddenly received a new firmware update. Not a virus. A... modification.

Their cameras began to stream video. Not of the airfield. But of General Sika's compound. Live feed.

And then, the signal boosted. It blasted out on an open frequency, the one the local military band used.

"Maya, pipe that to Sika's command radio," Alex said.

"Done."

General Sika, five miles away, heard the buzz of drones over his radio net. He looked at his radar. He saw the red swarm over the swamp. But his video feed showed him the sky over his own headquarters.

"Assassins!" Sika screamed over the open channel. "They are attacking the HQ! Fire! Fire at will!"

From the hills surrounding Sika's compound, the General's heavy AA guns erupted. Tracers tore into the sky.

But the real swarm was over the airfield.

The AA guns, seeing no targets on their radar, held fire. But the "Confetti" protocol Alex had uploaded made the drones emit a heat signature identical to a Russian helicopter.

Sika's men weren't shooting at bugs. They were shooting at ghosts.

And the real drones, confused by the GPS spoofing, started dropping their payloads early, bombs meant for the runway, harmlessly into the trees.

"It's a decoy play!" Sanjay shouted, laughing wildly, as a bomb exploded harmlessly in a banana tree. "You made them fight the invisible man!"

"Get the planes in the air!" Alex commanded.

The engines of the cargo jets roared. They lumbered down the dirt strip, heavy with the weight of the King's Blood.

One drone, smarter than the rest, broke the spoof. It corrected its path. It dove for the lead plane.

"Contact!" Maya yelled.

Alex didn't type. He grabbed a handset from the console.

"Sika! One breakaway! Vector 2-7-0!"

In his compound, Sika heard it. He had one battery of mobile AA left. He didn't aim at the sky. He aimed at the vector Alex gave.

WHOOSH.

A missile streaked across the sky, five miles away, and intercepted the drone just as it was about to strike the cockpit of the lead plane. The drone vaporized.

The lead plane lifted off, clawing for the sky. The second followed. The third.

The swarm, seeing the prey escape, broke off.

The airfield was clear.

Alex leaned against the console, wiping sweat from his forehead. His heart was hammering a frantic rhythm against his ribs.

"Package is away," Sanjay said, breathless. "We have the Cobalt. We have the... Ore."

Alex looked at the screen. The red blob of the mine was now linked to Baltimore with a pulsing green line.

He hadn't just bought a commodity. He had forged a private alliance. He had turned a warlord into a business partner. He had used a decoy strategy to defeat a corporate hit squad.

He had Expeditionary Force.

"Mr. Rivera," Sika's voice came over the radio. It was no longer cold. It was... warm. "You have strange ways, Commander. But my road is open."

"And your pumps are on order," Alex said. "My engineers are enroute."

"Then," Sika said, "we are in business. Safe travels."

The radio clicked off.

Alex looked at the jungle. The sun was setting, painting the sky in bruised purples and oranges.

He realized what they had just done.

Corporations spent billions on lobbyists. Nations spent trillions on armies.

He had spent twenty thousand dollars on software upgrades and one plane ticket.

He had bypassed the gridlock. He had gone into the gray zone.

And he had come back with the fuel that ran the world.

"Sanjay," Alex said, picking up his bag.

"Yeah, boss?"

"Find that goat," Alex said. "I think we're eating it tonight."

Sanjay grinned. "With fava beans?"

"With fava beans," Alex said.

They walked toward the waiting chopper. The rotors spun up, drowning out the sounds of the jungle.

Alex looked back one last time. The "failed state" of Kivu.

It wasn't failed. It was just inefficient.

And inefficiency was just an opportunity for a Commander.

***

Lesson Learnt:

- Military Doctrine: Expeditionary Warfare & The FOB. You don't conquer territory to occupy it; you conquer it to create a Forward Operating Base. The goal is power projection. You establish a beachhead, secure the logistics, and use that position to project force into the next theater.
- Financial Doctrine: Sovereign Arbitrage (The Gray Zone). The highest returns are not found in the efficient markets of the West. They are found in the "Gray Zones", failed states, conflict regions, chaotic markets, where Institutional Capital cannot go due to ESG rules and compliance fears.

- The Play: Don't buy the ETF. Don't buy the stock. Build a Private Treaty. Go to the source. Partner with the warlord/supplier. Provide the missing logistics (security/transport/processing) in exchange for the commodity at a massive discount.

The Insight: You are not an investor. You are a Merchant Sovereign. You privatize the supply chain. By going where others fear to go, you become the bottleneck of the world's economy. You don't dig the gold; you own the road it travels on.

Chapter 18: Sovereign Legacy

Location: The National Archives | The Rotunda for the Charters of Freedom | 14:00 Hours

The air in the Rotunda was cold, recycled, and smelled of floor wax and old paper. It was the smell of history that had been laminated.

Alex Rivera stood with his son, Ben, in front of the glass case that held the original Constitution of the United States. The document was faded, brown, and fragile. The ink was fading, a whisper of a rebellion that had birthed a superpower.

"It looks like a grocery list," Ben said, shoving his hands into his pockets and looking spectacularly unimpressed. He was sixteen, wearing a hoodie. He said, "Article One. Section Two. Boring."

Alex sighed. The patience of a saint was a prerequisite for fatherhood, but raising a teenage successor apparently requires the strategic reserves of a four-star General.

"It's not a grocery list, Ben," Alex said, keeping his voice low, respecting the hushed reverence of the room. "It's the source code of the country. It's the Operating System for our lives."

"It's buggy," Ben said, pointing at a glass case. "Look at the amendments. They had to patch it, what, twenty-seven times? If I shipped software that needed twenty-seven patches on Day One, I'd get fired."

Alex looked at his son. Ben was smart. Painfully smart. His brain processed data in ways Alex's military-trained mind couldn't always follow. But his wisdom... his wisdom was buffering.

"Code evolves," Alex said. "The world changes. The OS has to be patched."

"Whatever," Ben said, turning away from the Constitution. "Can we go now? I promised my friends I'd hit the mall. They're waiting in the food court."

"We're not leaving yet," Alex said. "We're here to discuss the patches to our family OS."

Ben groaned. The sound was a long, suffering vowel. "Dad, if this is about the Bugatti, the answer is yes. I need it. It's essential for my clout."

"You have a BMW," Alex said. "You have a driver. You go to a school that costs more per year than most people earn in a decade. You do not need a two-million-dollar car."

"It's not about the car," Ben argued, whipping around to face him. "It's about the grind. If I show up to the meet in the BMW, I'm just 'that rich kid.' If I show up in the Bugatti, I'm a legend. It's about establishing dominance."

Alex looked at his son. He heard the words, dominance, grind, legend, mixed with the vocabulary of a sociopath.

He realized with a cold pit in his stomach that he was losing the war.

He had fought the banks (Chapter 1). He had fought Vane (Chapter 12). He had fought the warlords of Kivu (Chapter 17).

But he was losing the battle for his son's soul.

"I'm creating a monster," Alex whispered.

"What?"

"Ben," Alex said, stepping closer. "I have built a Sovereign Fortress. I have built an Empire of capital. But I haven't built a Constitution for you. I haven't defined the terms of your engagement."

"Terms?" Ben laughed nervously. "Dad, you sound crazy."

"Listen to me," Alex said, his voice dropping into the register that had silenced barracks of angry soldiers. "Rich kids die, Ben. They don't die of hunger or malaria. They die of boredom. They die of meaninglessness. They live on substances, because life is too easy."

Ben looked at his shoes. The bravado slipped a notch.

"You're building a fortress," Alex continued. "I'm building the walls. But if I put you inside those walls without a mission, without a purpose... you become a zoo animal. You become a tiger in a cage who eats because he has nothing to hunt."

"So... no Bugatti?" Ben asked, looking up.

"The Bugatti is a toy," Alex said. "A Sovereign Commander doesn't play with toys. He pilots machines."

"I don't want to be a Commander," Ben said, a flash of anger breaking through. "I want to be a streamer. I want to make content. I want to build things in Minecraft and sell them to idiots. That's what I'm good at."

Alex stared at him. Minecraft.

"Okay," Alex said slowly. "We need to go to The Bunker."

"Now? But the food court!"

"The mall is closed," Alex lied, taking Ben by the elbow. "We have a boot sequence to initiate."

***

Location: The Bunker | The Legacy Chamber | 16:00 Hours

The Bunker had been remodeled. Or rather, a new wing had been excavated. The "Legacy Chamber" was not filled with servers or tactical maps. It was lined with bookshelves. Real books. Leather-bound histories of empires that had fallen.

JD sat at a circular table made of a single, massive slice of a California Redwood tree. He looked like a king holding court in a treehouse.

"Alex," JD said, looking up from a massive book titled 'The Decline of the Venetian Republic'. "You brought the Prince."

"I brought the problem," Alex said, sitting down. Ben slumped into a chair, pulling out his phone.

"No phones," JD said sharply.

Ben froze. He looked at his dad, then at JD. He dropped the phone on the table.

"We are here to discuss the single greatest failure of the wealthy class," JD said. He closed the book with a heavy thud. "The Lottery Winner Syndrome."

He pointed at Ben. "That boy is a lottery ticket. You, Alex, you are the winning numbers. But what happens to the ticket after the money is claimed?"

"It gets thrown away," Ben said, surprisingly articulate.

"Often," JD said. "Or it gets burned. The curse of wealth is that it removes Necessity."

He stood up and walked to a whiteboard that was strangely empty.

"Nature designed us to struggle," JD said. "We are designed to hunt, gather, build, protect. When you remove the struggle, when you give a sixteen-year-old a debit card with no limit, you break the human operating system."

"So I can't buy him a car?" Alex asked.

"You can buy him a car," JD said. "But you cannot give him Access. There is a difference."

JD drew a circle on the board.

"This is what most families do," JD said. "They put money, in a pile, in the center of the room. The kids stand around the pile and take what they want. It's a free-for-all. It creates entitlement. It creates sibling rivalry. It creates parasites."

He drew a second circle, this time with a wall dividing it.

"This is the Dynastic Model," JD said. "The way the Rockefellers, the Rothschilds, the Medici operated. They didn't leave money. They left Institutions."

He looked at Ben. "Do you know what an Institution is, kid?"

"Like a school?" Ben asked.

"It's a set of rules," JD said. "A Constitution. The Rockefellers didn't get trust funds just for being born. They had to meet the metrics."

"What metrics?" Ben asked, skeptical.

"Metrics of Competence," JD said. "Metrics of Contribution."

JD opened a folder on the table. He slid a document to Ben.

"This is the Family Constitution," JD said. "Alex, this is the software patch you need to write."

Ben picked up the document. It looked intimidating. Legal font. Dense text.

"What is this?"

"It's your charter," Alex said. "Ben, listen to me. The money I have made... it's not your money. It's the family's capital. You are a custodian of it."

"A custodian?"

"Like a park ranger," Alex said. "The ranger lives in the park. He enjoys the beauty. But his job is to protect it so the next generation can enjoy it too."

"If you want to drive the Bugatti," Alex continued, "you have to pitch the Board of Governors."

Ben laughed. "The what?"

"The Family Council," JD said. "Sanjay, Maya, and I sit on it. Your mother sits on it. You have to pitch us."

"Pitch you what?"

"A plan," Alex said. "A use of capital that increases the Sovereign Power of the family. It could be a business. It could be an investment. It could be a charitable initiative."

"But what if I just want to be happy?" Ben asked, his voice rising. "What if I just want to make YouTube videos?"

"Then you pitch us a business plan for a media network," Alex said calmly. "Show us the ROI. Show us the growth potential. Show us you are a Commander, not a consumer."

Ben stared at his father. "That's cold, Dad."

"It's necessary," Alex said. "Love is for the home, Ben. The bedroom, the dinner table, the hugs. Business is for the boardroom. If you mix them up, you destroy both."

"I'm sixteen," Ben said.

"And I was forty before I learned this lesson," Alex said. "I lost thirty years."

Ben looked down at the document. He read the first line.

ARTICLE I: THE RIGHT TO RESOURCE. All family capital is held in trust. Access to capital requires a qualifying mission statement.

"So," Ben said, thinking. "If I want to start a gaming studio..."

"You pitch us," Alex said. "You show us the design documents. The market analysis. The team. If it's a good investment, you get the capital. If it fails... you lose the capital, but you keep the lesson."

Ben's eyes narrowed. He was calculating. He was a gamer; he understood risk/reward mechanics.

"So..." Ben said slowly. "It's like... a raid boss? I have to form the party and execute the strategy to get the loot?"

Alex looked at JD. JD suppressed a smile.

"Exactly," Alex said. "Life is the raid. We just provide the gear."

"And if I don't want to raid?" Ben asked. "If I just want to... chill?"

"Then you get the Citizen Dividend," Alex said. "A basic income. Enough to live comfortably. Enough for a nice house, a nice car. But not enough for the Bugatti. Not enough for the private jet."

"The loot is for the winners," Ben whispered.

"The loot is for the builders," Alex corrected.

Ben put the document down. He looked at the Constitution in the glass case, no, he looked at the Family Constitution in his hands.

"It's a game," Ben said.

"It's the only game that matters," Alex said. "And it's a permadeath server. Your character dies, the account continues. Your choices echo down the lineage."

"What if I lose the money?" Ben asked. "What if I blow the raid?"

"Then you reboot," Alex said. "You start a Level 1 character. You don't get deleted. You just get... de-leveled."

Ben looked at his phone, sitting on the table. He didn't pick it up. He looked at JD.

"So," Ben said. "I can't have the Bugatti."

"Not yet," JD said. "Not until you build a car company that makes the Bugatti obsolete."

Ben grinned. A shark-like spark that Alex recognized immediately. It was the same look Alex had seen in the mirror.

"I have an idea," Ben said. "For the pitch."

"I'm listening," Alex said, his heart racing.

"Alpaca wool," Ben said. "Sanjay's stupid llamas."

Sanjay, who was standing in the corner, dropped his sandwich. "They are not stupid! They are the future of fiber optics!"

"Whatever," Ben said. "But I can market it. I can make Alpaca Swag the hypebeast of the decade. I can build a brand."

He looked at his father. "Is that a business?"

Alex looked at JD.

"It's a business," JD said. "It has viral potential. It has scalability."

"Then write the pitch," Alex said. "Friday. 0900 Hours. The Board convenes."

Ben stood up. He actually looked... excited. Not for the money. But for the challenge.

"I need a team," Ben said. "Can I hire Sarah?"

"Sarah's a lawyer," Alex said.

"Exactly," Ben said. "She handles the contracts. I handle the vision."

"Approved," Alex said.

Ben walked toward the door, then stopped. He looked back.

"Hey, Dad?"

"Yeah?"

"The Constitution," Ben said, tapping the document. "Can I add an amendment?"

"Which one?"

"The freedom to suck," Ben said. "If I try a raid and wipe, I want the guarantee I don't lose my citizenship. I don't want to be cut off."

Alex felt a warmth in his chest that had nothing to do with the servers.

"Amendment One," Alex said. "Failure is tuition. You never lose the citizenship."

Ben nodded. "Cool."

He walked out, walking with a bit of a strut. The strut of a man on a mission.

***

Location: The Bunker | The Legacy Chamber | 20:00 Hours

The sun had set. The Bunker was quiet, except for the hum of the cooling system.

Alex and JD sat alone at the Redwood table. The bottle of scotch from the "victory" chapter (15) sat between them, half-empty.

"He's going to be dangerous," JD said, pouring the last inch. "He has the hunger."

"He has the arrogance," Alex said.

"Arrogance is just unproven confidence," JD said. "He'll crash a few times. That's good. It's better to crash at 20 with a safety net than at 50 with nothing."

Alex looked at the document Ben had left behind.

"Do you think this will work?" Alex asked. "The Constitution? The Family Council?"

"It's the only thing that works," JD said. "Look at history. The Romans used inheritance to buy votes. They corrupted the republic. The British used inheritance to buy titles. They stagnated the empire."

He swirled the scotch.

"The families that lasted?" JD continued. "The ones who left Rules rather than Assets? The Hapsburgs? The Rothschilds? They lasted because they treated the family like a corporation. They didn't promote on tenure. They promoted on competence."

JD looked at Alex.

"You're not building a bank account for your kids, Alex. You're building a Culture."

Alex thought about the "Core Processor" (Chapter 12). The algorithm that rejected the noise.

"I'm building a filter," Alex said. "The money is the noise if they don't have the character to hold it."

"Precisely," JD said. "This is the final piece of the OS, Alex. You have the Terrain (Infrastructure). You have the Logistics (The Bunker). You have the Firewall (The Trust)."

He tapped the Family Constitution.

"This is the User Interface. This is how the humans interact with the machine."

He stood up.

"It's time to go home, Commander."

"To Elena?"

"To Elena," JD said. "She is the first signatory. If she doesn't sign, the document is just paper."

Alex nodded. He knew Elena. She would sign. She would probably add her own amendment about cleaning up rooms or doing homework.

But she would sign.

Because she knew what Alex was just realizing.

Money without purpose was a bomb. It was dangerous.

But money in the hands of a Commander... Commander by Commander?

That was an Empire.

And empires last long, after the Kings are buried.

Alex walked out of the Bunker, feeling lighter than he had in weeks.

He had defeated the Harvest. He had conquered the Grid. He had survived the Legal Siege (Chapter 16).

But today?

Today he had defeated the most dangerous enemy of all.

He had defeated Entropy.

***

Lesson Learnt:

- Military Doctrine: The Rules of Engagement (ROE). An army without ROE is a mob. It destroys itself. A military legacy is built on discipline, standard operating procedures, and a clear chain of command that is based on competence, not birthright.

- Financial Doctrine: Sovereign Legacy (The Family Constitution vs. The Trust Fund). Traditional inheritance is the "Sugar Crash", giving resources to entities unprepared to process them, leading to systemic failure (addiction, laziness, ruin).

    - The "Family Office" Model: Treat the family wealth as a Venture Capital Firm. The heirs are Founders, not Trust Funders. They must pitch a "Mission Statement" (The Charter) to a Board of Governors to access capital.

- The Citizenship Clause: The distinction between Equity (lifestyle funds for everyone) and Control (sovereign capital for the builders). Heirs who wish to pursue the "grind" or artistic paths receive a safe, comfortable "Citizen's Dividend" but do not get control of the "Empire." Control is reserved for those who accept the risk of Command.

The Insight: You do not leave your kids money; you leave them a Code. You leave them a Challenge. The greatest gift you can give the next generation is not a safety net, but a worthy adversary to prove themselves against. Wealth is not what you give them; it's the system that forces them to grow.

Chapter 19: The Wealth Command OS - Live Deployment

Location: The Bunker | The War Room | 10:00 Hours

The sound of money is usually silent. It is the hum of a server rack, the whisper of a fiber line, the gentle rhythmic clicking of a mouse.

At 10:03 AM, the sound changed.

It started as a low-frequency vibration in the floorboards of The Bunker. Then it became a shriek. Not from the machines, but from the humans.

Maya screamed. It wasn't a word; it was a raw sound of disbelief, like watching a plane crash into a playground.

"SYSTEMIC SHOCK!" Maya yelled, throwing her keyboard away. "The Treasury curve is inverted! The yields are spiking to 15%!"

On the main wall-screen, the global map, which usually glowed with gentle green indicators of flow, suddenly turned a uniform, sickening crimson.

It wasn't a sector crash. It wasn't a tech bubble bursting.

It was The Harvest.

The global debt market, the lifeblood of the modern world, was having a cardiac arrest.

"Quantitative Tightening," JD said, his voice calm. He was standing by the coffee machine, which was gasping and dying. "The Fed pulled the plug. The liquidity that propped up the fake stock prices is gone."

Sanjay was spinning in his chair, clutching three phones. "Gold is up! Bitcoin is down! The Algo-bots are panic-selling everything! They're hitting the bid-ask spread on everything!"

"Shut down the Alphas," Alex commanded, his voice cutting through the noise.

He didn't panic. He had spent three months running simulations of this exact moment. He had drilled his team until their hands bled.

"The outside world is entering the 'Red Zone'," Alex said, walking to the center console. "They are going to experience fear like they have never known it. ATMs will freeze. Banks will halt withdrawals. Credit cards will decline."

He sat down. "We do not freeze. We engage."

"Engage what?" Maya asked, her eyes wide, reflecting the red light of the room. "Everything is crashing! Our paper net worth just dropped 40%!"

"Our paper net worth dropped," Alex corrected. "Our real wealth is just waking up."

He typed a command. PROTOCOL: LIVE DEPLOYMENT.

"Sanjay, open the floodgates," Alex ordered.

"Which ones?"

"All of them."

***

Location: The Baltimore Mall | Server Farm (The Citadel) | 11:30 Hours

The city of Baltimore was dark. Not just the lights; the energy of the place had died. The "Harvest" had reached the streets. People were realizing that their credit was gone, their money was frozen, and their cards were just plastic.

The Baltimore Mall was an island of light.

Inside the "Citadel", the server farm Alex had built in the ruins of the Sears, the hum was deafening. The servers weren't just processing data; they were processing the life of the new economy.

Alex stood on the mezzanine, watching the security feeds. The perimeter was surrounded by a crowd.

Not a rioting mob. A desperate mob. They weren't looting; they were begging. They held phones that didn't work. They held children who were cold.

"Alex," Sanjay's voice came in his ear. "The crowd is getting restive. They see the lights on. They know we have power."

"I know," Alex said. "Send in the distribution teams."

"We don't have food!" Sanjay yelled. "We have servers!"

"We have the Rivera Credit," Alex said. "Activate the vending machines."

He had installed them in the lobby. Machines that looked like ATMs, but didn't dispense cash. They dispensed Credits. Digital units backed by the Cobalt contract and the Aether energy production.

They couldn't buy iPhones. But they could buy bread from the local bakers who had agreed to accept the Credit.

"Opening the outer doors," Maya said. "Commander, this is a security risk. They could rush the server floor."

"They won't," Alex said. "Because the lights are on."

Suddenly, the security alarm blared. BREACH: REAR DOCK.

***

Three black vans screeched to a halt outside the loading docks. They didn't have markings. They had makeshift assault ladders and heavy bolt-cutters.

"Who is that?" Maya asked.

"Vane," Alex said, his jaw tightening. "He can't crash the market, so he's going to crash the hardware."

Men in tactical gear poured out of the vans. They weren't local looters. They moved with precision. They set charges on the main power transformers that fed the Citadel.

"He's cutting the cord," Alex whispered. "He wants to plunge us into darkness with the rest of the city."

"Defense grid is offline!" Maya shouted. "We can't activate the automated sentries! They're physically severing the line!"

"Use the backup," Alex said. "The Peacocks."

"The Peacocks are decoy servers, Alex! They don't shoot!"

"Not those Peacocks," Alex said. "The Alpacas."

Sanjay had installed a perimeter defense system based on modified warehouse drones. They were bulky, ugly, and heavily shielded.

"Deploy the herd," Alex commanded.

In the parking lot, the chaos of the crash met the chaos of the farm. Six heavy-lift drones, painted with the stylized logo of a grazing llama, dropped from the roof of the mall.

They didn't shoot bullets. They shot webbing.

High-tensile, rapid-deploying net cannons engulfed the sabotage team. The men were tangled, lifted off the ground, and unceremoniously deposited in the beds of pickup trucks that belonged to the very "looters" Alex had hired as a perimeter guard.

The looters, seeing the "bad men" wrapped up like burritos, started cheering.

"Vane is fleeing," Maya reported, watching the drone feed. "He's pulling back."

"He realizes he's fighting a war in 4D while he's stuck in 2D," Alex said. "Secure the transformers. Get the grid back online."

***

Location: The Bunker | The War Room | 14:00 Hours

The screens were still red, but a new data stream was overlaying them. Green numbers.

"Alex," Sanjay said, his voice trembling with excitement. "The banks are frozen. The credit markets are toast. But... the peer-to-peer lending protocol we built for the Aether contractors? It's exploding."

He turned his screen. It showed a graph of a new currency. R-CREDIT.

"People are trading," Sanjay said. "They are trading their old cars, their old jewelry, their labor for R-Credits. Because R-Credits can buy food and power."

"Because R-Credits are backed by the Cobalt," Alex said.

"Exactly," JD said, walking up to the console. He was holding a glass of water. "While the world fights over paper money, you have cornered the market on Reality."

He pointed to the red screen of the stock market.

"Vane is ruined," JD said. "He shorted the market, expecting a crash. He got one. But he can't collect his winnings because the clearinghouse is offline."

"And he can't cover his shorts," Alex said, "because the stocks aren't trading."

"Precisely," JD said. "He is trapped in a burning theater with no exits."

Alex looked at the phone on his desk. It was ringing. The private line.

"Hello, Martin."

"Alex! Oh god, Alex! Thank god!" Martin's voice was a high-pitched keen of terror. "My accounts are frozen! The bank is closed! I can't get cash for my wife's medication! The ATM just ate my card! What do I do?"

"Martin," Alex said calmly. "Do you have any physical assets?"

"I... I have gold coins. A few. And a watch."

"Bring them to the mall," Alex said. "To the North Gate. I have a kiosk open."

"You... you're buying gold?"

"No," Alex said. "I'm buying Paper."

"Paper?"

"Deeds," Alex said. "Mortgage notes. Car loans. The promissory notes that the banks are dumping because they think the world is ending."

He looked at Maya. "Execute Project Carpet."

Maya typed. ACQUIRING TOXIC ASSETS: CONFIRMED.

The banks, desperate for any liquidity, were auctioning off their loan portfolios at ten cents on the dollar. They were selling the mortgages on people's homes.

Alex was buying them.

"Why?" Martin asked, sobbing now. "Why buy the debt?"

"Because," Alex said, "tomorrow, when the lights come back on, people are going to need to pay their mortgages. And they're going to pay them to me."

"And if they can't?"

"Then they pay rent," Alex said. "To me."

He hung up.

"General," Alex said, looking at JD. "We just bought the neighborhood."

"You just bought the city," JD corrected. "You just became the bank of last resort."

"The Sovereign Bank," Alex said.

He looked at the screen. The red crash was fading into a steady, rhythmic pulse. The chaotic algorithms of the market had broken. They had been replaced by the logic of the Wealth Command OS.

It wasn't magic. It was logistics.

While the world fought over the illusion of wealth, Alex had bought the mechanisms of survival.

"Sanjay," Alex said. "Open a line to the Treasury."

"The Treasury?"

"Tell them we are re-injecting liquidity," Alex said. "Into the R-Credit system. We are backing our digital dollars with Cobalt and Power."

"You're pegging the dollar?" JD asked, raising an eyebrow.

"I'm offering an alternative," Alex corrected. "An upgrade."

He watched the screen. The R-Credit exchange rate stabilized against the dying dollar. It found a floor.

"The system is working," Alex said.

He felt a profound sense of quiet. It wasn't the silence of the grave, but the silence of the engine room. The hum of a machine that was doing exactly what it was designed to do.

"It's beautiful," Maya whispered, watching the clean lines of the new protocol. "It's not chaotic. It's... orderly."

"Order is the product of Command," JD said.

Alex looked at his hands. They weren't shaking.

He had done it. He hadn't just survived the crash; he had ridden it. He had used the momentum of the collapse to propel himself forward.

"Sir," Sanjay said. "Apex Energy stock is halted at zero. They are delisting it."

"Let them," Alex said. "I own the debt. I own the power plant. I own the Cobalt. The stock is just a souvenir."

He stood up.

"Where are you going?" JD asked.

"Home," Alex said. "The power is stable. I need to check on Elena and the kids."

"Are you going to tell them?" Maya asked. "That you just bought the bank?"

"No," Alex said, smiling. "I'm going to tell them I fixed the lights."

He walked to the door of The Bunker. The heavy steel shielding felt lighter.

Behind him, the screens glowed. Not red. Not green.

A deep, steady, royal blue.

The Sovereign OS was deployed.

Lesson Learnt:

Military Doctrine: Operational Continuity. In the event of a catastrophic event (Black Swan), the goal is not to retreat, but to re-establish command and control on the new terrain. The unit that can adapt its logistics to the new reality survives; the unit that tries to hold the old line is overrun.

Financial Doctrine: The Liquidity Crisis & The Sovereign Floor.

The Event: Systemic "Harvest" scenarios (debt deflation, currency collapse) freeze traditional assets (stocks/bonds) because the clearinghouses fail.

The Trap: Most investors hold cash, which becomes worthless or frozen. They hold "Gold," which they can't spend.

The Sovereign OS Response:

Own the Mechanism: Don't own the money; own the payment rail. (The R-Credit system/Cobalt-backed currency).

Buy the Toxicity: When the herd panic-sells assets for pennies (Mortgages, real estate debt), you buy the claim on the future reality. You become the landlord of the recovery.

Provide the Bridge: Issue private liquidity (credit) against real assets when the public markets are offline.

The Insight: Wealth is not what you hold when the world is normal. Wealth is what you hold when the world breaks. A Sovereign doesn't fear the crash; he deploys his forces into the gap.

Chapter 20: The Next Command

Location: The Chesapeake Bay | Aboard "The Sovereign" | 06:00 Hours

The Chesapeake in October was painted in hues of brushed steel and soft bronze. The water was choppy, a rhythmic agitation that usually sent amateur sailors back to the dock with green faces and stained pants.

Alex Rivera stood at helm of The Sovereign, a converted trawler that looked less like a pleasure craft and more like a floating tank. It was ugly, functional, and reinforced with Kevlar hull plating that could withstand a torpedo or a particularly angry piece of driftwood.

He loved this boat. It didn't glide; it plowed.

"You're going to strip the gears if you keep fighting the wheel like that," Elena said.

She was sitting on the bench behind him, wrapped in a thick wool fisherman's sweater, holding a thermos of coffee. She looked... different. Not younger, exactly, but unburdened. The frantic tension that had usually lived in the corners of her eyes, the fear of the next tuition payment, the anxiety of the market downturn, had evaporated. It had been replaced by a calm, steely confidence.

She looked like a woman who knew the exits were unlocked.

"I'm not fighting it," Alex said, easing the throttle slightly. "I'm sensing it. You have to feel the water through the keel, not just stare at the compass."

"You sound like JD," Elena said, smiling. "Is he coming today?"

"He is," Alex said. "He's bringing Sanjay. Sanjay apparently has a 'major announcement' regarding the Alpacas."

The radio crackled.

"Command, this is Base. You have a visual on the starboard bow. Over."

Alex looked up. A sleek, black cutter of a boat was tearing across the bay, skipping over the waves like a stone thrown by a giant. At the helm stood Sanjay, wearing a tuxedo t-shirt and a captain's hat, waving frantically.

Beside him, JD stood with his hands clasped behind his back, looking like a monument observing the ocean.

"They're here," Alex said.

"Are we going to race?" Elena asked, her eyes sparkling. "Because I have twenty dollars on Sanjay."

"Sanjay is racing his ego," Alex said. "I'm just holding course."

He eased The Sovereign into a wide turn, the diesel engine thrumming a contented bass note beneath the floorboards. As he turned, he looked back at the coast. The skyline of Baltimore was rising in the distance, a cluster of glass and steel that had, six months ago, been a graveyard.

Now, it was the heartbeat of the new economy. The Baltimore Node, the "Citadel", hummed silently from there, providing the digital spine for half the Eastern Seaboard.

They had done it. They had actually done it.

***

Location: The First National Bank | Main Branch | 14:00 Hours

The bank was a temple to the old ways. High ceilings, marble floors, and the smell of polish and fear.

Alex walked in, dressed in a blazer and jeans, with Elena on his arm. He wasn't here for a loan. He was here for an eviction.

Not of people. Of a system.

Martin Sterling was packing a box. He looked smaller than Alex remembered. The impeccable armor of his suits hung loosely on his frame. His face was gray, not from makeup, but from exhaustion.

The lobby was empty. The teller lines were unmanned. The irony was bitter: Martin had preached safety, yet the "Safe" system had collapsed, taking his career with it. The R-Credit system; the digital liquidity Alex had built, had rendered the traditional clearinghouses obsolete. People didn't come to banks to get money anymore; they came to them to deposit the deeds they couldn't afford to keep, in exchange for R-Credits to buy food.

Martin looked up as Alex's shadow fell across his desk. He flinched.

"Alex," Martin said. His voice was hollow. "Elena. I... I heard about the rescue package. The credit lines for the city."

"The city didn't need a bailout," Elena said gently. "They just needed a bridge."

Martin nodded, looking down at his box of personal effects, a framed photo of his kids, a stapler, a potted plant. "I tried to warn you, Alex. The Glide Path. I really thought it was the only way."

"I know," Alex said. "You were operating on the manual, Martin. You were using maps from the last century."

"And you?" Martin asked, a bitter edge creeping into his voice. "You bought the harbor. You bought the grid. You bought the debt of three nations. You didn't just beat the market, Alex. You ate it."

Alex walked to the massive windows that looked out onto the street. The world outside was moving again. Chaotic, messy, loud. But it was moving.

"I didn't eat it, Martin," Alex said, correcting him softly. "I just took control of the supply lines. I don't want to be the king. I just want to be the guy who owns the road."

"I'm unemployed," Martin said. "The board dissolved the institution this morning."

"The building is solid," Alex said.

Martin looked up. "What?"

"We bought it," Elena said. "Rivera Holdings acquired the deed an hour ago."

Martin blinked. "You... bought the bank? Why? To turn it into a server room?"

"No," Alex said. "We're turning it into a 'People's Server.' A hub for the R-Credit network. A place where people can come to trade their labor for credits without the predatory fees."

He looked at Martin. "I remember you said you were a logistics officer who liked to count rations. I need a logistics manager, Martin. Not a loan officer. A manager of flow."

Martin stared at him. The job offer wasn't charity; it was a salvage operation. It was a role where Martin's skills, his meticulous nature, his caution, his knowledge of regulation, were assets, not liabilities.

"I don't do crypto," Martin said, his voice trembling. "I don't do 'Alpacas.'"

"You don't have to," Alex said. "You just have to make sure the grandmas don't starve. You just have to make sure the road doesn't get blocked."

He placed a hand on Martin's shoulder. "You were right about one thing, Martin. We do need a glide path. Just not one that goes down."

Martin looked at Elena, then back at Alex. He put the framed photo back into the box, and then took it out again. He stood up, squaring his shoulders.

"The logistics of the people," Martin whispered. "I can do that."

"Good man," Alex said.

He walked out of the bank, leaving the old world behind. He didn't look back.

***

Location: The Bunker | The Observation Deck | 20:00 Hours

The sun was setting, casting long, bloody shadows across the floor of the Bunker. The team was gathered. Sanjay, Maya, Elena, Ben, and JD.

There was a cake on the central console. It had "Mission Accomplished" written in shaky icing.

"I have an announcement!" Sanjay yelled, bouncing on his toes. "The Alpacas!"

"We know, Sanjay," Maya groaned. "The fiber is insulated. We get it."

"No! Not that!" Sanjay said. "I bought the mountain. The whole mountain. The Alpacas are now a sovereign protectorate! We are issuing 'Llama Coins' backed by wool production!"

The room stared at him.

"It's a hedge," Sanjay defended. "If the internet crashes, everyone will need sweaters!"

JD chuckled. It was a deep, rumbling sound like distant thunder. He walked to the front of the room, standing in front of the massive screen that displayed the global map of the Wealth Command OS.

The map wasn't red anymore. It was a network of pulsing blue and gold lines. The "Harvest" had been reaped, and the fields were sown.

"Today," JD said, his voice quieting the room, "we mark the end of the beginning."

He looked at Alex. "The Boot Sequence is complete. The Firewall is configured. The Multi-Thread is stable. And the Legacy... is secured."

He tapped his chest. "My part in this operation is concluded."

"Quitting?" Ben asked, sounding shocked.

"Transitioning," JD corrected. "I am an old General, Ben. My war was the Cold War. Your father's war was the War on Terror. And this war... this was the War for Sovereignty."

He took off his rank insignia pins, the silver stars that had adorned his collar for fifty years. He placed them on the console.

"I cannot teach you how to fight the next battle," JD said. "Because the next battle will be fought in dimensions I can't see. Space. Mind. Biology."

He looked at Alex. "I'm handing the command to you, Alex."

Alex stood up. The weight of it didn't feel heavy. It felt like the handle of the trawler, grip, textured, ready for the sea.

"Who are we fighting now, Dad?" Ben asked. "Who is the enemy?"

"There is no enemy," Alex said, looking at his son. "Not anymore. When you are truly Sovereign, when you command your own logistics, there is no one left to fight."

He walked to the screen.

"The enemy was dependence," Alex said. "The enemy was the illusion of the Peace Dividend. The enemy was the idea that we had to settle for less than we were."

He looked at Elena. "We have the House. We have the Home. We have the World."

He tapped the screen. "And we have the OS."

"So we just... live?" Elena asked. "We just enjoy the peace dividend?"

Alex smiled. He wrapped his arm around her waist.

"No," he said. "The Peace Dividend is a lie, El. Peace is a pause. It's a breath between waves."

He looked at the map of the world. The lights of the Sovereign OS were twinkling like stars.

"The next command," Alex said, "is Expansion. Not of territory, but of capability. We take the OS public. We teach others how to de-brief their lives. We show them how to build their own forts."

"We franchise the rebellion?" Sanjay asked, grinning.

"We franchise the freedom," JD corrected.

Alex looked at the team. Maya was already coding the "Open Source" protocols. Sanjay was planning the launch of the "Llama Coin" IPO. Ben was drafting a new venture pitch; this one for real.

The system was running. It was alive. It didn't need him to steer it every second anymore. It had its own momentum.

"Then let's go home," Alex said. "I think I want to grill that steak I bought last month. The one that cost more than my first rent."

"Agreed," Elena said.

They walked out of The Bunker, leaving the screens humming.

JD stood alone for a moment. He looked at the map. The red was gone. The blue lights were expanding, branching out, connecting new nodes.

"Carry the fire," he whispered to the empty room.

He turned off the lights.

***

Location: The Rivera Residence | The Deck | 21:30 Hours

The night air was cool, crisp with the scent of burning leaves from the neighbor's yard. A sure sign of autumn, of the turning of the season.

Alex sat on the porch swing, a glass of scotch in his hand. He wasn't checking his phone. He wasn't checking the stock ticker. He was just listening.

The crickets. The distant hum of the highway. The breath of the woman he loved asleep inside.

Elena came out, wrapped in a blanket. She sat down next to him, resting her head on his shoulder.

"It's quiet," she said.

"It is," Alex said.

"Is it weird?" she asked. "Not... panicking?"

"It's not weird," Alex said. "It's just... readiness."

He took a sip of the scotch. The smoke curled up into the darkness.

"I used to think Command was about shouting orders," Alex said softly. "About driving people. About the weight of the world."

"It's not?" Elena whispered.

"No," Alex said. "Command is about stillness. It's about having the clarity to know that when the wave comes, you won't be crushed. You'll just ride it."

He looked at the dark silhouette of the trees at the edge of the yard. The terrain.

"We built a good life, Alex," she said.

"We built a sovereign life," he corrected.

He put his glass down. He put his arm around her.

"What's the next mission?" she asked, half-asleep.

Alex smiled into the dark. He thought of the world out there. The millions of people still running on the treadmills of the Peace Dividend Illusion, terrified of the Glide Path, waiting for someone to tell them they could be more.

He had the manual. He had the OS.

"The next command," Alex whispered, closing his eyes, "is to wake them up."

The wind picked up, rustling the leaves. The world turned, but the Sovereign held the line.

The end.

***

Lesson Learnt:

- Military Doctrine: Mission Command (The Intent of the Commander). The highest form of leadership is not micromanagement but establishing the "Commander's Intent." Once the intent is clear and the system is trained, the Commander can step back. The operation becomes self-sustaining. Success is not one man's victory; it is the culture that survives his departure.

- Financial Doctrine: The Sovereign Endowment vs. The Estate.

    - The Estate: A static pile of assets (houses, stocks, cash) that consumes the owner with maintenance, taxes, and fear. It is a fortress that you are trapped inside.

    - The Endowment: A dynamic flow of capital and purpose. A system (an OS) that generates resources independent of the owner's direct labor. An Endowment funds missions, not lifestyles. It creates a legacy of competence, not just consumption.

The Insight: You do not build wealth to "retire" (The Peace Dividend). You build wealth to "deploy" (The Second Command). The goal of Sovereignty is to reach a state where your capital works for you, creating the ultimate luxury of all: Time. The time to think, to lead, and to find the next mission. The war is never over; the Commander just moves to a higher observation deck.

Epilogue: The Third Command

Location: The Bunker (Now Known as "The Citadel") | Arlington, Virginia | 10:00 Hours

The Bunker had outgrown its name. What was once a dusty third-floor warehouse smelling of stale coffee and intrigue was now an underground cathedral of data. The "Citadel."

It stretched five stories underground, bored into the bedrock beneath Arlington. It didn't hum anymore; it sang. The sound of a million cooling fans working in harmony was a low, infrasonic thrum that vibrated in your teeth.

Alex Rivera stood on the mezzanine of Operations, looking down at the main floor. It was a sea of movement. Hundreds of operators, many of them young, kids who would have been flipping burgers or coding apps three years ago, now sat at dual-screen stations, managing the flow of the Wealth Command OS.

They weren't trading stocks. They were routing logistics for the new world.

"Traffic in the 'Amazonas' sector is spiking," Sanjay said, rolling his chair over. He was wearing a shawl. An actual, velvet cape.

"Why the shawl?" Alex asked, without looking away from his screen.

"It's the 'Alpaca Baron' look," Sanjay said, spinning. "The internet loves it. I'm a meme, Commander. A financially solvent meme."

Alex smiled. "Focus, Baron. The Amazonas sector?"

"They're trying to execute a massive withdrawal of credits," Sanjay said, his fingers dancing across the keys. "They're liquidating assets to buy land for the new farms. We need to increase the bandwidth on the South American bridge."

"Do it," Alex said.

"You know," Sanjay muttered, typing furiously, "three years ago, I had to beg a bank for a fifty-thousand-dollar line of credit. Today, I just moved fifty billion in digital credits to stabilize the Peruvian grain market."

He looked up. "It feels good. Being a Central Banker."

"We're not a bank, Sanjay," Alex corrected gently. "We're the logistics provider. We're the road."

"The road," Sanjay agreed. "And the toll booth."

Alex looked around the bustling floor. Down below, in the "Legacy Wing," he could see Ben. His son was now twenty. He wasn't wearing a hoodie and headphones. He was wearing a suit, tailored, sharp, and he was shouting at a team of architects.

"No! The tower needs to be taller! The symbol matters! If we're going to host the Global Sovereign Summit, the building has to scream 'We are here to stay!'"

Ben had founded Rivera Global, a construction firm that specialized in building "Sovereign-Ready" infrastructure. Fortified homes, micro-grid communities, defensible real estate. He had built it on the back of the "Alpaca" brand and the strength of the Rivera name. He was a builder.

Alex felt the warmth in his chest again. Not the heat of servers, but the heat of pride.

The OS was working.

But it wasn't enough.

***

Location: The Lincoln Memorial Reflecting Pool | Washington D.C. | 16:00 Hours

The crowd was... polite.

Two hundred thousand people stood on the National Mall. They weren't rioting. They weren't holding signs. They were holding smartphones, recording. They were quiet.

Alex Rivera stood on the steps of the Lincoln Memorial. Behind him, the Reflecting Pool rippled in the wind, reflecting the sky and the monument.

To his left sat the "Family Council." Elena. Ben. Sarah, now a corporate lawyer with eyes like flint. JD sat in a wheelchair now, a blanket over his legs, his face a map of beautiful wrinkles.

To his right sat the "Global Council." Leaders from the Kivu Republic. The new Prime Minister of the UK. The Tech Czars of the Pacific Rim.

They were here for The Sovereign Summit.

The world was changing. The "Harvest" of three years ago had reset the board. The old banks had survived, but they were no longer the masters of the universe. They were just big, slow dinosaurs eating the grass that the new, fast mammals, Alex's 'Commanders', didn't want.

Alex stepped up to the microphone. The feedback screeched, then died.

"Three years ago," Alex began, his voice amplified by a sound system powerful enough to shatter glass. "I stood in this city and was told that I was entering a managed decline."

A murmur ran through the crowd.

"I was told that my productive years were over. That I should accept the Peace Dividend. That I should fade away."

He looked at the cameras.

"I didn't listen."

"The financial industry sold a lie. They told us that the economy was a zero-sum game. That for one side to win, another had to lose. That for the middle class to be safe, the rich had to be protected."

He paused.

"But we learned something new. We learned that the economy is an ecosystem. And in an ecosystem, the only way to thrive... is to grow."

He pointed to the Reflecting Pool.

"For three years, we have operated the Wealth Command OS in private. We built the roads. We secured the supply lines. We defended the Home Territories."

"And now," Alex said, his voice hardening, "we are faced with a new enemy."

The crowd went silent.

"The enemy isn't a bank. It isn't a hedge fund. It isn't a rival nation."

"The enemy is Inertia."

"The Peace Dividend was a sedative," Alex said. "It put the world to sleep. We are waking up. But waking up the world is not a one-time event. It is a perpetual motion. You cannot stand still."

He stepped closer to the edge of the stage.

"We have built an Operating System that works. An OS that turns a pensioner into a Commander. A system that allows a teacher in Ohio to become a Sovereign Investor. A system that allows a farmer in Kivu to own his logistics."

He tapped a tablet on the podium.

"Today, I am not announcing a new product."

"I am announcing a General Order."

He paused for effect.

"Wealth Command OS is going Open Source."

The reaction wasn't a cheer. It was a gasp. Two hundred thousand people inhaled at once.

"The code," Alex said. "The algorithms. The protocols. The 'Kernel.' We are giving it to the world. For free."

Behind him, Elena didn't flinch. Ben didn't blink. But the financial reporters in the press pit started screaming questions.

"You're giving it away? How will you monetize it? What about your advantage?"

"Quiet!" Alex commanded, using the Voice.

The silence returned.

"Our advantage was never the code," Alex said. "Our advantage was the Doctrine. The mindset. The refusal to accept the Glide Path."

"The algorithms are just tools. You can give a man a hammer, but that doesn't make him a builder. You can give a man a gun, but that doesn't make him a soldier."

"We are giving the world the hammer," Alex said. "We are teaching them to build."

"This is The Third Command."

He looked out at the sea of faces.

"Your First Command was your career. You served a system."

"Your Second Command is your life. You built your own system."

"Your Third Command is your legacy. You teach the system to others."

Alex smiled. It was a warrior's smile.

"We are recruiting. Not for an army. But for a Corps of Engineers. We are looking for people who want to build the roads. People who want to own the pipes. People who are tired of being passengers."

He pointed at the Washington Monument in the distance.

"The Peace Dividend is over. The Sovereign Era begins now. And it begins... with you."

He stepped back from the mic.

The silence held for one second. Two.

And then, the roar started. It didn't come from the front. It came from the back. From the families. From the young people. From the aspirants of the world.

It was a roar of engines starting.

JD leaned over in his wheelchair, gripping Alex's arm.

"You just started a war, Alex," JD whispered, chuckling softly.

"No," Alex said, watching the flags snapping in the wind. "I just conscripted an army."

***

Location: The Boat "The Sovereign" | Chesapeake Bay | 20:00 Hours

The sun was setting, painting the water in streaks of molten gold and deep purple.

The "Sovereign" cut through the water, smooth and fast. The hum of the engine was a constant, reassuring note.

Elena stood at the stern, the wind whipping her hair. She was holding two glasses of champagne.

"You know," she said, handing one to Alex. "The world is going to hate you."

Alex took the glass. "Why?"

"Because you broke the system," Elena said. "You took the power away from the elite. You handed it to the mob."

"I didn't hand them power," Alex said. "I handed them responsibility. It's not the same thing."

"They'll figure that out," Elena said, smiling. "The smart ones will."

Alex looked at the horizon. Where the sky met the water. The world was vast. It was chaotic. It was dangerous. And for the first time in history, it was free.

"Do you think it worked?" Alex asked. "The Epilogue? Did we stick the landing?"

Elena looked at him. "We didn't land, Alex."

"We didn't?"

"No," she said, tapping her glass against his. "We took off."

Alex smiled. He looked back at the receding shoreline of Washington. The Citadel was underground. The Summit was history. The speech was uploaded, being dissected, analyzed, and, in a million basements, downloaded.

The code was out there. The "Third Command" was running in the wild.

He thought of JD. He thought of Sanjay and his cape. He thought of Ben and his skyscrapers.

And he thought of the reader.

The person who was holding this book.

Alex looked up, seemingly staring at the reader through the fourth wall.

"You think you're ready?" Alex asked softly. "You think you have the Kernel?"

He took a sip of champagne. The bubbles burst on his tongue.

"It's not about the money," he said. "It was never about the money."

"It's about the Terrain."

He pointed at the open water.

"It's a big map. Go claim your corner."

***

Location: The Bunker (The Citadel) | The Core Server Room | 23:59 Hours

The room was cold. Dark.

A single red light blinked on the master console.

SYSTEM STATUS: LIVE. GLOBAL NODES: 1,402,394. NEW RECRUITS: 4,512 SINCE SPEECH.

A cursor blinked on a blank command line.

USER_INPUT_REQUIRED.

IDENTITY: [EDITED]

WELCOME, COMMANDER.

INITIATING BOOT SEQUENCE...

THE THIRD COMMAND BEGINS.

A Note on the Journey Ahead

You have read the chronicle of 'The Second Command'. You have seen how a retired military officer transformed his life, his family, and his wealth using the principles of Wealth Command OS.

But this is not a story to be merely read. It is a code to be executed.

The financial landscape has shifted since the "Harvest" of the AI era. The Peace Dividend, the idea of a safe, managed decline, is no longer a viable strategy. It is a death sentence.

The principles in this book are not fiction. They are doctrine.

- The Core Processor: Define your values, not your risk tolerance.
- The Firewall: Protect your assets from the "Gliding Path" mentality.

- The Expeditionary Force: Deploy capital into asymmetric opportunities.
- The Legacy: Build institutions that outlast you.

You do not need a Bunker. You do not need a Sanjay or a Maya.

You need a Command.

You need to decide that you will no longer be a passive consumer of the economy. You will no longer accept the "Glide Path." You will no longer treat your midlife years as a decline.

You will be a Commander.

The tools are out there. The terrain is waiting. The enemy: Inertia and Fear, is always present.

It is time to stop looking for the Peace Dividend.

It is time to launch the Next Command.

Boot Up. Go, do it!

Acknowledgments

Writing this book has been a campaign unlike any other. It required not just research, but a fundamental shift in my own heart and mind, a forging of a new lens, to see the world. To write honestly about warfare and finance is to speak two ancient, powerful languages, each with its own grammar of risk, sacrifice, and consequence. I found; I could not create this perspective alone. In truth, I am merely the scribe, humbled by the task of translating the quiet, echoing voices that have taken residence in my soul.

My deepest salute is to the men and women of the Special Operations community. You taught me that 'logistics' is not a dry corporate term. It is the whisper of a helicopter in the night, the weight of a ration in your pack, the certainty of a satellite link when everything else is static. You taught me that logistics is a synonym for life, for hope, for the promise that no one gets left behind. The discipline I learned from you, the sacred focus on the enablers, the unseen architecture of success, is the very spine of this book. You know who you are, and I carry those lessons every day.

To the financial warriors who operate in the quiet corners, far from the screaming headlines of "Wall Street." You are the ones who understand that real wealth isn't captured in a frenzy; it is built in the silent, patient spaces. You master the boring, brutal, beautiful math of supply and demand, the logistics of capital. You showed me that the balance sheet is a battlefield, and that true victory comes from securing the high ground of cash flow and controlling the supply lines of assets. Your quiet resolve is the hidden engine of this narrative.

To my family, my first and final command. You are the unwavering home base for a heart that too often deploys into the deep. You have endured the long silences, the distracted stares, the weekends lost while 'the mission' was underway. You have held the line at home, so I could attempt to hold a line on these pages. This book is a piece of territory won, but it is yours more than it is mine. Your love is the only non-negotiable asset I will ever need.

And finally, to you, the reader, who now holds this volume. Thank you. Thank you for pausing in the noise of the world to pick up this weapon, this tool, this map. You are not a spectator. By choosing to engage, you are stepping onto the field. The strategies within are inert without your courage to enact them. This book is a trusted piece of gear passed to you. The mission, now, is yours. Move with purpose.

About - The Digital Annex

The concepts of "The Sovereign Wealth Command OS," the "Three-Theater War," and the specific protocols (The Peacocks, The Empty Fort, The Black Room) are explored in greater depth at the interactive annex.

There, you will find:

- The Kernel Quiz: Discover your true financial personality.
- The Terrain Map: A visual guide to finding your asymmetric opportunities.
- The Boot Sequence Checklist: A 90-day plan to initiate your Second Command.

The Digital Annex

You've read the intelligence report. You've seen how Commander Rivera built his Sovereign Wealth OS. You've seen him defeat the Peace Dividend Illusion, outmaneuver the Warlord of Kivu, and survive the Harvest.

But reading about war and fighting it are two different things.

In the Bunker, we don't just read manuals. We run simulations. We test the operator before we deploy the unit.

You have the hardware (your assets). You have the terrain (the market). Now, it's time to install the software.

Welcome to the Digital Annex. This is your staging ground. Below, you will find the three core tools of the Wealth Command OS, expanded and operationalized for your own deployment.

Don't just scroll through this. Engage with it. If you are truly ready for your Second Command, these tools will wake you up. If you aren't, they might scare the hell out of you.

Good luck, Commander.

Tool 01: The Kernel Quiz (Discover Your Operator Profile)

Most financial planners ask you: "What is your risk tolerance?"

This is a useless question. It asks how you feel about losing money, not how you function as a human being. A man with a high pain tolerance can still be a bad investor if his brain is wired wrong.

In the Wealth Command OS, we don't care about your pain threshold. We care about your Value Algorithm. We need to know who is driving the vehicle.

Take the quiz below. Be honest. If you lie, you're only hacking yourself.

Scenario A: The Burning Warehouse. You own a warehouse. It catches fire. The smoke billows high. You see a truck parked out front.

- Option Alpha: You rush inside with a bucket of water, hoping to save a stack of dusty boxes in the corner.
- Option Bravo: You run to the truck, hotwire the ignition, and drive that truck to the rival warehouse across town.

Analysis: If you chose Alpha, you are The Logistician. You value the preservation of specific assets over the survival of the system. You are likely hoarding cash, gold, or "safe" stocks that are actually rotting. You confuse ownership with hoarding. If you chose Bravo, you are The Speculator. You are willing to burn it all down for a chaotic upside. You have high energy but low discipline. You need a leash.

Scenario B: The Blockade. A massive storm is coming. The enemy has blockaded the harbor. Your supplies are trapped.

- Option Alpha: You order your men to fortify the warehouse. You build walls. You prepare to starve until the storm passes.
- Option Bravo: You order your men to build a raft. Not to flee, but to float over the blockade to trade with the open ocean beyond.

Analysis: If you chose Alpha, you are The Defender. You play "Not to Lose." You will likely end up with a pile of dust that is safe, but worthless. If you chose Bravo, you are The Architect. You understand that flow is more important than static assets. You are ready to build the bridge.

Scenario C: The Prisoner Break. You are captured. The enemy General offers you a deal.

- Option Alpha: You take the deal. You take the safe job in the mines. It guarantees survival for you and your family.
- Option Bravo: You take the deal, but only to steal the keys to the armory on your way out.

Analysis: If you chose Alpha, you are The Civilian. You are still operating on "Safe Mode." You will be eaten by the system eventually. If you chose Bravo, you are The Sovereign.

You understand that you cannot be free if you are dependent on the enemy's food, even if you eat well.

Your Kernel Profile:

- Logistician + Defender: You are stuck in "Safe Mode." You need to read Chapter 11 (Boot Sequence) immediately.
- Speculator + Architect: You have high capability but no grounding. You need to build a "Firewall" (Chapter 14) or you will crash.
- Sovereign: You are ready for Second Command. But check your ego.

***

Tool 02: The Terrain Map (Scouting the Battlefield)

The retail investor looks at the surface. They see a stock price, a P/E ratio, a product on Amazon. This is looking at the skin of the battlefield.

The Sovereign Commander looks at the bones. They look for the pipes, the wires, the chokepoints.

The Terrain Map is a methodology for scanning your local economy (or any global market) to find the invisible value. It is about identifying Layer 2 Assets, the infrastructure that powers Layer 3 (Consumer Products).

How To Read the Map (The 3 Layers of Value)

- Layer 1: The Substrate (The Dirt)
    - What is it? Physical resources. Land, water, rare earth metals, spectrum bandwidth, power generation.
    - The Insight: Everyone fights over the gold in the river. The Sovereign buys the claim to the river bend.
- Layer 2: The Logistics (The Pipe)
    - What is it? The transport of value. Fiber optic backbones, shipping routes, railroad spurs, payment processing rails, cold-storage logistics.
    - The Insight: This is the "Sweet Spot." It is boring, invisible, and essential. When a major website goes down, the company that owns the cables in the ground

still gets paid. When retail stores close, the companies that own the warehouses continue to thrive.

- Layer 3: The Application (The Skin)
    - What is it? Brands, Apps, Retail, Consumer Discretionary.
    - The Insight: This is the "Noise." It is volatile, crowded, and fashion-driven. The Sovereign only plays here if they own the Layer 2 pipe underneath.

Exercise: Map Your Zip Code Take your own neighborhood or city. Don't look at the house prices. Look for the flow.

1. The Chokepoint: Is there a bridge that, if it collapsed, would starve the city? Who owns it?
2. The Invisible Pipe: Where is the internet actually coming from? (Hint: It's not the WiFi router. Follow the black wires on the pole).
3. The Storage: Where does the food sit before it hits the shelf? Who owns the refrigeration?

The Play: Find the Layer 2 asset that is undervalued. If the bridge is rusty, the land is worthless. If the bridge is gold, the land is just a bonus. Buy the bridge.

Tool 03: The Boot Sequence Checklist (The 90-Day Campaign)

This is your actionable plan. This is how you go from a civilian reading a book to a Commander deploying an OS.

WARNING: Do not skip days. This is an algorithm. If you skip the diagnostics, you will crash the system.

Phase 1: The Extraction (Days 1-30)

Objective: Clear the RAM. Remove the bloatware.

- Day 1-7: The Financial Autopsy
    - Log every single asset. Stocks, bonds, 401(k)s, cash.
    - Identify the "Emotional Holdings." The stock you inherited from your dad. The mutual fund your buddy sold you.
    - Mark them for liquidation. They are cancer.
- Day 8-14: The Subscription Purge
    - Cancel Netflix. Cancel Spotify. Cancel the gym membership you don't use.
    - Sanjay's Rule: If it's recurring, it's a leak. Plug it.
    - Calculate the "Cash Flow Delta." How much free cash did you just reclaim?

- Day 15-30: The Asset Segregation
    - Separate your assets into three piles:
    - Pile A (Home Theater): 6 months of expenses. This is your Ammo. Do not touch.
    - Pile B (Expeditionary): Capital you can afford to lose 100% of. This is your Risk Capital.
    - Pile C (Legacy): Long-term holds (Real Estate, Trusts). These stay buried.

Phase 2: Fortification (Days 31-60)

Objective: Build the Firewall. Configure the Trust.

- Day 31-40: The Legal Buffer
    - Consult a lawyer (Do not use your brother-in-law). You need a pro.
    - Discuss the "Black Knight" structure (Chapter 16).
    - Goal: Move your personal name off the Deeds. Become a Tenant of your own life.
- Day 41-50: The Debt Restructure
    - Refinance high-interest consumer debt into lower-rate asset-based debt (if possible).
    - If you cannot, attack the highest interest loan first. The "Kill the Enemy" protocol.

- Day 51-60: The Intelligence Setup
  - Open a separate checking account for your "Expeditionary" capital.
  - This account is not for buying groceries. It is for war.
  - Do not link it to your primary debit card. Isolate it.

Phase 3: Deployment (Days 61-90)

Objective: The First Strike.

- Day 61-70: Terrain Scouting
  - Use your "Terrain Map" skills. Find the Layer 2 asset.
  - Do not buy yet. Just watch. Identify the Chokepoint.
- Day 71-80: The Sniper Shot
  - Take 10% of your Expeditionary Capital (Pile B).
  - Deploy it into your chosen Terrain play.
  - Rule: If you don't feel the fear in your stomach, the position is too small.
- Day 81-89: The Monitor
  - Do not look at the price every day. Look at the Logic.
  - Is the pipe flowing? Is the supply chain moving?

    - If the Logic holds, stay in. If the Logic breaks, get out. Don't argue with the market.

- Day 90: The Evaluation
    - Review your 90 days.
    - Is your stress level lower?
    - Is your "Home Theater" (Pile A) still full?
    - If yes, you have successfully booted the OS.

Final Order: The system is live. You are no longer a consumer. You are a node in the network.

Welcome to the war, Commander.

Glossary of Terms

Asymmetric Warfare: A strategy where a smaller, weaker force uses unconventional tactics to exploit the vulnerabilities of a larger, stronger adversary. In finance, this means competing on terrain where large institutions cannot effectively operate (e.g., small private deals, complex logistical solves, regulatory arbitrage).

Black Swan Event: A highly improbable, high-impact event that lies outside the realm of normal expectations. The Wealth Command OS is designed not to predict these, but to be antifragile, to gain from them.

Boot Sequence: The process of initializing your Wealth Command OS, moving from a passive, saving-oriented state to an active, deploying state. Involves liquidating "safe" but low-yield assets to fuel strategic capital deployment.

Center of Gravity: The source of strength, balance, or leverage in any system. In wealth creation, identifying the enemy's (e.g., a competitor's, the market's) and your own center of gravity is critical for focused action.

Digital Annex, The: The living, evolving component of the Wealth Command OS. Contains the models, templates, tools, and frameworks referenced in the narrative. Access is provided separately, as a static book cannot contain a dynamic system.

Empty Fort Strategy: A deception tactic where appearing weak and exposed invites the enemy into a trap. In sovereignty, it means leveraging privacy and opacity to allow competitors to underestimate you until it's too late.

Expeditionary Theater: One of the Three Theaters of the wealth war. Dedicated to high-risk, high-growth offensive operations (e.g., angel investing, venture capital, strategic private equity). Capital here is allocated with the expectation of volatility and potential loss.

Firewall: A defensive mechanism, both digital and psychological, designed to filter noise, block malicious attacks (cyber, legal, psychological), and protect the core systems of your sovereignty.

Force Multiplier: A factor that dramatically increases the effectiveness of a given force. In the Wealth Command OS, your experience, network, discipline, and intelligence apparatus are force multipliers applied to your capital.

Home Theater: One of the Three Theaters of the wealth war. The fortress. Dedicated to absolute security and the non-negotiable obligations of life (primary residence, family safety, essential income). This theater is defended with zero-tolerance for risk.

Kernel (Value Algorithm): The core processing unit of your personal OS. It is the set of fundamental beliefs and values (e.g., Flow, Autonomy, Impact) that filters all decisions. Aligning your financial strategy with your Kernel prevents internal conflict and systemic failure.

Legacy Theater: One of the Three Theaters of the wealth war. The diplomatic corps. Dedicated to multi-generational impact, influence, and building structures that outlast you (trusts, foundations, enduring enterprises). Operates on a doctrine of strategic patience.

Logistics of Sovereignty: The principles governing the movement and deployment of capital. Emphasizes velocity and mobility over static accumulation. True wealth is measured by how quickly and effectively you can project financial force.

Narrative Injection: The deliberate seeding of information (often via media) by market participants to create a public perception that serves their financial position (e.g., spreading fear to drive down a stock they have shorted).

OODA Loop (Observe, Orient, Decide, Act): A military decision-making cycle developed by Colonel John Boyd. The key to victory is processing this loop faster than your competition, creating confusion and reactionary behavior in the adversary.

Sovereignty: The supreme authority over your own economic and personal fate. The state of being unassailable by external systems (corporate employment, predatory financial products, inflationary erosion). The ultimate objective of the Wealth Command OS.

Terrain: The environment in which financial warfare is conducted. Includes physical terrain (real estate, infrastructure), digital terrain (data flows, IP addresses), and human terrain (networks, regulatory landscapes). Victory comes from terrain mastery, not just asset accumulation.

Three-Theater War: The strategic framework separating your assets and objectives into three distinct operational zones: Home Theater (Defense), Expeditionary Theater (Offense), and Legacy Theater (Diplomacy). Prevents the fatal error of using defensive capital for offensive bets.

Wealth Command OS (Operating System): The integrated framework of mindset, strategy, and tools for building sovereign wealth. It treats financial life with the rigor of a military campaign, emphasizing command, intelligence, logistics, and strategic terrain analysis over product selection and passive investing.

Resources & Further Reading

This section is intentionally brief. The true resource isn't found in books, but in the system, you build and the intelligence you cultivate. The following are not endorsements, but points of departure for your own terrain analysis.

On Strategy & Mindset

- Sun Tzu, The Art of War (multiple translations). Read not for ancient tactics, but for the philosophy of asymmetric advantage and psychological dominance.
- Robert Greene, The 33 Strategies of War & The 48 Laws of Power. Frameworks for understanding human dynamics as terrain.
- Nassim Nicholas Taleb, Incerto series (The Black Swan, Antifragile, etc.). The foundational texts on

navigating uncertainty and building systems that gain from disorder.

- James Stockdale, Thoughts of a Philosophical Fighter Pilot. On the synthesis of Stoicism and command in the face of extreme adversity.

On Systems & Economics

- Ray Dalio, Principles & The Changing World Order. Macro-economic cycles and the systematic principles behind Bridgewater's success.

- Andy Grove, Only the Paranoid Survive. Strategic inflection points from the former Intel CEO; a masterclass in sensing shifts in the terrain.

- W. Edwards Deming, Out of the Crisis. The source code for quality management and systemic thinking, borrowed from by Japan to rebuild its industrial base.

- The Sovereign Individual by James Dale Davidson & Lord William Rees-Mogg. A prescient (and controversial) look at the impact of the digital revolution on sovereignty, wealth, and power.

On Intelligence & Decision-Making

- Richards J. Heuer Jr., Psychology of Intelligence Analysis. The CIA manual on cognitive biases, structuring analysis, and challenging established mindsets.

- Shane Parrish, The Great Mental Models series. Frameworks for clear thinking across disciplines.
- The U.S. Army / Marine Corps Counterinsurgency Field Manual (FM 3-24). A source for understanding complex, adaptive systems and the principles of building legitimacy, applicable to building ventures and alliances.

On Logistics & Execution

- Eliyahu M. Goldratt, The Goal. A novel about process and bottleneck management that will change how you see any operational system.
- Stephen Bungay, The Art of Action. How military mission command (Auftragstaktik) principles can be applied to business to bridge the gap between strategy and execution.

Important Note: Read these not to adopt their conclusions, but to reverse-engineer their thought processes. Your most critical resource is your own lived experience, your network, and the intelligence apparatus you build. These books are calibration tools, not command manuals.

Review Request

Dear Reader,

Thank you so much for choosing **'The Second Command'**.

If you enjoyed it, may I humbly request you to share your thoughts and review on Amazon?

Your review goes a long way for the readers to find this book on Amazon and enjoy reading like you. Even a few sentences about what resonated with you can make a huge difference.

Your support means more than you know. Thank you for being part of this journey.

With gratitude,
Paolo Crisp

www.ingramcontent.com/pod-product-compliance
Lightning Source LLC
LaVergne TN
LVHW100251210926
848480LV00003B/893